ABEAR

FOR CHILDREN

David W. Andrews, Ph.D.
Lawrence Soberman, M.Ed.

Illustrated by Ray Yost

Published by Family Support Systems
Eugene, Oregon

Parents

Abear is two books in one. The introduction to *Abear for Parents* explains the most effective way to use *Abear for Children*. Please read the Introduction to *Abear for Parents* before reading *Abear for Children*.

To Our Families

Acknowledgements

We would like to thank everyone who helped bring "the bear" to life. First was the scheming of Sue Doescher and Gini Aducci who helped coin the name Abear. Then, the artistry and imagination of Ray Yost who gave the bears form and face. All along the way we received constant encouragement and support from our families.

We would like to acknowledge the decades of research by professionals in child development and education on which the material in this book was based. In addition, we thank those that imparted this knowledge to us -- our teachers and mentors.

Finally, we express our gratitude to all of the children with whom we have worked and played over the years. Any of our insights into the world of children come from them.

Contents

CHAPTER 1

WE SELDOM HAVE ENOUGH FOOD

The sun was shining and it was a warm, glorious day. "What a day for gathering berries!" shouted Abear.

"It's a wonderful day!" Mom exclaimed. "I seldom have days this beautiful for picking berries."

Abear thought about what his mother said, "I <u>seldom</u> have days this beautiful for picking berries." He liked the sound of the word "seldom." He didn't know what it meant, but he liked how it sounded.

He really wanted to ask Mom about the word "seldom," but he was afraid she would think that he wasn't very smart.

Abear <u>did</u> know that the sun was shining brightly every time he went berry picking. "I seldom have days this beautiful for picking berries," repeated Abear.

He decided that seldom must be the same as "always." Abear always had days this beautiful when he went berry picking.

But Abear was forgetting that it rained often during berry picking season. When it was raining Abear didn't go with his parents to pick berries.

Abear's mom picked berries in the rain most of the time. She hardly ever had beautiful days for berry picking, and that is what she meant when she used the word seldom.

2

There were plenty of berries in the woods this time of year. It didn't take long for Abear and his mom to fill their baskets.

"We are lucky to have so much food," said Abear.

"Yes we are," answered Mom. "It has been a very good year for getting food."

They had gathered more than enough food for the family. Abear and Mom walked slowly toward the bear caves on the mountain.

"Can I go to Bearly's cave and play?" asked Abear. "Of course," smiled Mom, "you've been a very good helper."

Abear ran as fast as he could to Bearly's cave. He was disappointed to find that Bearly was not at home.

Bearly's mother noticed the berry stains on Abear's fingers. "Have you been picking berries?" she asked.

"Oh yes, and just like every year, we <u>seldom</u> have enough to eat," said Abear. He was happy to have a chance to use his new word so soon.

Bearly's mom was suddenly sad. She thought about how terrible it must be for Abear and his family not to have enough food.

Early the next morning Mom saw someone coming up the trail to their cave. As they got closer she could see that it was Bearly and his mother. They were pushing a cart loaded with nuts, berries, and honey.

"Welcome to our cave," said Mom, taking a long, puzzled look at the cart of food.

Bearly's mom began to explain, "We know how hard your family has been trying to gather food, and this cart is for you."

Not knowing what to say, Abear's mom managed a smile and said softly, "Well....thank you." Without another word Bearly and his mother turned and started quickly down the mountain trail.

Abear's mom was very confused. Why would anyone bring them so much food? And, why would they think that they even needed food? This time of year they had more food than they could possibly eat.

"Abear," she called. "Do you know anything about this food?" Abear looked at the cart loaded with food. He seemed as puzzled as his mother.

"No Mother," he said, more confused than ever. But later, he began to think that maybe he didn't really understand what he was saying when he used the word "seldom."

His mother could tell that something was bothering him. "Abear, are you sure there isn't something you would like to tell me?" asked Mom.

Abear was afraid that his mother would be angry, so he just kept saying that he didn't know anything about the food.

Abear and Mom stood for a long time looking at the cart of food.

"Well," said Mom, "we'll just have to push this cart of food down the mountain and explain to Bearly and his mom that there must be some mistake."

Abear couldn't stand it any longer. He had to tell his mother what he had said to Bearly's mom.

"Mom, I do remember telling Bearly's mom that we <u>seldom</u> have enough food."

Mom stared at Abear for several seconds. She didn't know what to do.

There, in the cart, was all the food. In front of her was Abear, confused and frightened. They looked at each other thinking, "What should we do now?"

CHAPTER 2

THE CLIFF

"Dad!" shouted Abear as he entered the cave. "Dad, where are you?"

"I'm in the kitchen," called Dad.

Abear and Bearly walked as fast as they could to the kitchen. They were in a hurry and wanted to run, but they knew it was against the rules to run in the cave.

Abear's dad was just beginning to make his famous fish cakes for dinner when the two little bears came storming into the room. "Dad, can Bearly and I go fishing at Big Creek Waterfall?" asked Abear.

"Well," said Dad, "it's a long walk to that big waterfall. I'm not sure that I want you cubs going all that way without a big bear."

Abear thought for a minute. Then without warning it just came out, "Mom lets us go alone!"

He knew that he wasn't telling the truth. And, he knew he would be in big trouble if Dad asked Mom about the waterfall.

"I guess you can go," he hesitated, "but only because your mother lets you. You know the rules. I especially want you to remember the rule about climbing up the cliffs near the waterfall."

"I know, I know," said Abear. He felt like he was always being reminded of the rules.

"I won't climb up the cliffs. I won't get too close to the waterfall. And, I will be home before dark," he said, repeating Dad's most important rules.

"Yipee!" Abear and Bearly were on their way. Eager to get to the fishing hole, they walked briskly down the path until they came to two trails. Both trails were very narrow and went in slightly different directions through the tall trees of the forest.

Abear and Bearly couldn't wait to get to the bottom of the waterfall, but they couldn't remember which trail to take.

"I think it's this one," said Bearly pointing to one of the trails.

"Me too," Abear agreed, and they were off again.

After walking for what seemed like a very long time, they came to the river.

"We made it!" shouted Abear.

But Bearly looked worried. He didn't recognize anything. The river looked wider. There wasn't a pool for fishing. And, he couldn't see the waterfall. "Abear, I think we made it to the wrong place."

"Listen," said Abear. "I think I hear it."
As they got quiet, Bearly could also hear the sound of falling water.

The two bears ran along the river toward the sound of the water. Suddenly, just before they came to the edge of the big cliff, they stopped.

"Oh no," cried Abear, "we are at the <u>top</u> of the waterfall. The fishing pool is at the <u>bottom</u>."

Abear and Bearly carefully walked to the edge of the cliff. Peeking over they could see that it was a long way to the bottom and quite steep. There wasn't enough time before dark to walk back through the forest to the other trail. The bears didn't know what to do.

"Hey, Abear," called Bearly, "I think I found a way down."

Bearly had walked along the cliff until he was very close to the top of the waterfall. He could see a tiny, winding trail leading down the cliff. The trail was very small and very close to the falling water.

"I don't know," frowned Abear looking at the trail. "It's very steep, and we promised my dad we wouldn't climb the cliffs."

Bearly thought for awhile, "Didn't we tell your dad we wouldn't climb <u>up</u> the cliff? Well, we're not going to climb up, we are going to climb <u>down</u>."

Abear knew that his dad didn't want him climbing up or down the cliff, but Bearly was right. They only had said they wouldn't climb <u>up</u> the cliff.

Abear was first to try going down the trail. He was nearly half-way to the bottom when he called up to Bearly, "Come on, it's easy."

Just then his feet began to slip. He stumbled and fell very close to the edge of the waterfall. When he tried to stand up, the rock that his foot was on came loose.

"HELP!" he called. It was too late. He fell toward the waterfall and landed in the fishing pond below.

14

Bearly was frightened. He ran faster than he had ever run through the forest, back to the trail leading to the bottom of the waterfall. When he finally got through the forest, there was Abear sitting on the edge of the pond, soaking wet.

"Are you all right?" asked Bearly.

"I think so," whined Abear. "My foot hurts a little, but I think I'll be fine." Abear was very wet.

The sun was setting, and he began to get cold. "We'll never get home before dark," thought Abear.

It was dark by the time Abear reached his cave. Dad and Mom were both waiting outside. They were very worried. Abear was wet and covered with mud. His foot still hurt as he limped toward them.

Dad picked Abear up and helped him into the cave. Dad covered him with a blanket while Mom fixed a wrap for his foot.

"Now," said Dad, "I think it's time for you to tell us what happened."

Slowly, Abear began to tell his story. Before he spoke he thought, "What should I say? What will happen to me now?"

CHAPTER 3

THE NEW BEAR AND THE STILTS

Abear couldn't wait to get home. He had promised Bearly that he would come over to play as soon as the family returned from the honey hunt.

Abear and Bearly had been best friends since they were tiny cubs. Only one empty cave separated their families. They liked to play together, eat together, and go on long hikes together. It seemed as if the cubs were nearly always together.

Abear skipped quickly along the ridge of Bear Cave Mountain on his way to Bearly's. He was moving so fast that he almost didn't see the cub standing outside of the empty cave.

The cave had been empty for so long that he was surprised to find someone there. At first the bear seemed very tall and much older than Abear. But after taking a closer look, Abear could see that the bear was standing on something. It looked like she was standing on two sticks.

Abear walked a little closer.

"Hi there," said the new neighbor, "my name is Bearette."

Abear said hello but kept staring at the sticks that held Bearette high in the air.

"My name is Abear," he was finally able to say. "What are you standing on?"

"Oh," said Bearette, "these are called stilts. My dad and I use them to look down into tree stumps that might have honey inside."

"They look like great fun!" said Abear. "Could I try them, please?"

Bearette was happy to see that there were other bears on the mountain, and she was quick to let Abear try out the stilts.

At first Abear had trouble keeping his balance on the stilts. But, soon he was able to walk a long way down the path. Walking on the stilts was as fun as it looked. Abear and Bearette spent most of the afternoon taking turns on the stilts.

Abear was having such a good time that he forgot about going to Bearly's. That is, until he saw Bearly coming up the trail. He sure hoped Bearly wasn't going to be angry.

"Hi Bearly," said Abear, "I was just learning how to use Bearette's stilts."

Bearly grumbled, "Hello." He didn't look happy, and he was watching Bearette closely. He hadn't met Bearette, and he wasn't sure what to say.

"Oh, Bearly," said Abear, suddenly remembering that Bearly didn't know Bearette, "This is Bearette. Her family just moved into the empty cave."

Abear and Bearette took turns with the stilts and had a wonderful time. Bearly just kept standing and watching. Not once did he ask to have a turn on the stilts. Not once did Abear or Bearette offer him a turn.

After watching for what seemed like a very long time, Bearly turned and started back down the trail.

Abear saw him leaving and yelled after him, "Hey Bearly, why don't we play at your cave tomorrow?"

Bearly didn't answer.

The next day Abear awoke at daybreak. He had all day to play with Bearly. He hoped Bearly wouldn't be angry about Bearette and the stilts. Abear was sure that Bearette would have given Bearly a turn, if Bearly had only asked for one.

When Abear got close to Bearly's cave he could hear what sounded like cubs playing. It was still early in the morning. Who could be at Bearly's cave this early?

Then, under a tree, beside the entrance to Bearly's cave, Abear saw Bearly and Bearette playing a game of marbles.

Abear was a little disappointed. He had hoped that Bearly would go with him to the river. But, he decided, he would be just as happy playing marbles.

"Hi there," said Abear as he walked toward the two bears.

They didn't even look up from the marbles.

"Can I have a turn?" Abear continued.

Again, the cubs acted like they heard nothing. Maybe they just didn't hear him. Or maybe they just didn't want to play with him.

Abear was getting angry.

He was almost ready to go home when Bearette said, "Abear, would you like a turn?"

"Sure!" shouted a much happier Abear. Bearette and Bearly watched as Abear rolled the marbles. When Abear had taken his turn, Bearly and Bearette began playing again, as if Abear wasn't around.

Now, Abear really didn't know what to do. Should he ask for another turn? Should he tell Bearly and Bearette how angry he was getting? Should he suggest that they all go to the river? Or, should he just go home and be alone? He kept wondering, "What should I do?"

CHAPTER 4

GRANDPA'S PAINTINGS

"Is everyone ready?" called Dad into the cave. He wondered what was keeping Abear's little brother, Weebear. Finally, Weebear came out of the cave dragging a very large pack filled with toys.

"Weebear!" cried Mom spotting the tiny bear struggling to carry the heavy pack. "I don't think you're going to make it to Grandma's cave carrying all of those things. It's a very long way and the mountains are steep."

Even though it was a long way to Grandma's, Abear and his parents were anxious to be on their way. They helped Weebear unpack some toys and were finally on the trail.

They were just past the green valley when Dad began his speech. It was the same speech he gave to the cubs every time they traveled to Grandma's.

"Please listen," he started. "I want you to remember the rules at Grandma's house. Some of the rules are the same as we have at home and some are different. But most of all I want you to remember that it is Grandma's house, and her rules."

The little bears said nothing, but they thought about Grandma. She never had any rules. She always let the little bears do whatever they wanted.

Grandma was waiting in front of her cave as they walked up from the valley.

"Oh, look how much you've grown," said Grandma as she hugged each of the young bears and pinched their furry cheeks.

Abear and Weebear didn't like to have their cheeks pinched, but they tried to smile. "Can we play in the back of the cave?" asked Abear as soon as Grandma loosened her grip on his cheek.

Grandma had lots of old, neat things way back at the end of her long, narrow cave. The cubs were anxious to see what interesting things they could find.

"Let's visit with Grandma first," said Mom. She wasn't happy with Abear for asking to play before he even said hello to his grandmother.

"Mom," whined Weebear, "we really want to play."

"Pleeeease!" added Abear with his own tiny voice.

"Oh dear," said Grandma to Mom, "let the little fellows have some fun."

Abear and Weebear were out of sight before Mom or Dad could say a word. The little bears knew that their parents wouldn't argue with Grandma.

The cubs were anxious to explore Grandma's treasures in the back of the cave. Scattered throughout Grandma's things the little bears found several beautiful paintings. They were mostly paintings of bears -- big bears, little bears, all kinds of bears.

In a dresser drawer they found some old brushes and paint. "I remember," said Abear suddenly, "Grandpa bear was an artist. I bet these were his brushes, and this was his paint."

"I wonder if these old brushes and paint still work?" said Weebear.

"There's only one way to find out," answered Abear. "Let's try them."

The cubs couldn't find any paper so they decided to add to the paintings that they had found. Abear drew a big hat with a flower on one painting. Weebear just scribbled on all of the paintings he could reach.

"Oh, no!" cried Grandma when she entered the back of the cave. "Those were my favorite paintings," she sighed. She was very sad, but it was difficult for her to be angry with the young cubs.

"Let's put these things back," said Grandma wiping a tear from her eye. She noticed that nearly every painting had been ruined.

Mom called the young bears to dinner just as the last painting was being returned to its place.

"What were you doing in the back of the cave?" Dad asked when the cubs sat down for dinner. The little bears looked at each other. Then they looked at Grandma. Grandma was staring into her bowl of soup. She didn't say anything.

"Playing," said Abear.

"Yea, just playing," added Weebear.

Grandma just kept staring into her soup.

"Grandma," said Dad after dinner, "I've really been wanting to see Grandpa's old paintings. Maybe the cubs would like to see the paintings of their mother when she was a cub."

"Great idea," said Mom. "I'll get the paintings."

"Please don't!" said Grandma trying to protect the cubs. "Nobody really wants to see those old paintings."

"Sure we do," said Mom as she headed toward the back of the cave. She couldn't understand why Grandma wasn't interested in the paintings. She usually loved to pull out Grandpa's art work.

Mom came back to the front of the cave with a paw full of ruined pictures. She was very angry.

"Mother, how could this have happened?" she cried staring down at the paintings.

Before Grandma could answer the cubs lowered their heads and mumbled, "We're sorry!"

Mom was too upset to speak. Her favorite paintings, the only ones that were left from Grandpa's collection, were ruined.

"I think it's time for us to go home," said Dad. Mom was still silent.

They all kissed Grandma goodbye. The walk home was long and quiet.

Once home the cubs were quick to get into their pajamas and hop into bed. They knew that it wouldn't be long until Mom and Dad came in to talk about the day. They were right. They each thought to themselves, "What should we say? What should we do?"

CHAPTER 5

WHAT A MESS

One rainy day Abear sat quietly in his room putting together a puzzle. Abear was very good with puzzles and soon he was down to the very last piece, but he couldn't find it. He looked under the piles of dirty bandannas in the cor-ner. He looked through his scattered collection of rocks. He even moved some of the art work lying around on the floor.

It was no use!

"This room's a mess," he moaned. "I guess I should clean it before I lose something else."

He spent the rest of the day cleaning. He picked up all of the clothes that were scattered on the floor. He made his bed, and he put away all of his toys, except for the ones that he crammed under the bed and into the closet.

"Whew, what a job," he thought as he inspected his clean room.

He stood tall beside his door when he heard Mom coming. Mom walked right past Abear, but she said nothing about his clean room. "Maybe she didn't notice, or maybe it wasn't clean enough," thought Abear.

The next day Abear was out of bed at daybreak. He had decided to once again clean his room, this time it would be better than ever. He would clean it so well that his mother wouldn't be able to miss it.

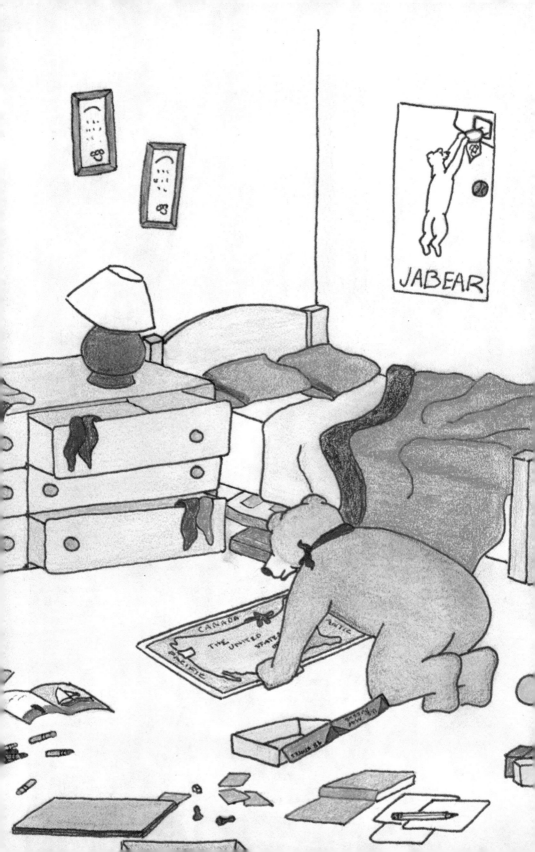

This time he cleaned his closet, got all of the toys out from under his bed, and even folded all of his bandannas. Abear usually just stuffed his bandannas into a drawer, all wadded up.

His room sparkled. He couldn't wait for his mom to see it. She would be so happy. There might even be a reward for being such a good room cleaner.

"Abear!" called Mom.

"Yes Mom," he answered as he hurried to the front of the cave. Proudly, Abear stood in front of his mom waiting for her to praise him for cleaning his room.

"Son," she began in a very serious voice, "I found your toys on the path again. How many times have I told you how dangerous it is to leave your toys where other bears walk?"

Abear couldn't believe what he was hearing. How could Mom be angry after what he had done with his room? "It's not fair," he thought, but he didn't complain. Instead, he kept his room spotless for a whole week. Mom would certainly be proud when she found his spotless room.

Mom walked past his room at least ten times everyday. Somehow, she just never looked inside.

Now, Abear was more than disappointed. He was angry. He decided to find Bearly and get some advice.

Dad came home while Abear was away. Walking past Abear's room he noticed something very different. He went inside and marveled at what he saw. He couldn't believe his eyes. This was the cleanest he had ever seen Abear's room.

"Abear," he called.

"I just saw him walking down the path to Bearly's," answered Mom.

"Come and look at Abear's room," called Dad. He wanted Mom to be sure and see the good job Abear had done.

"What a great surprise!" said Mom. "I didn't even ask him to clean his room. I wonder how long it has been this way?"

By the time Abear got to Bearly's he was more upset and disappointed than ever. He didn't know that Mom and Dad had discovered his clean room.

"What's the problem?" Bearly asked when he saw Abear's long face.

Bearly listened to Abear and decided he had the perfect plan. "If they didn't notice when it was clean, then maybe you should just mess it all up. I mean really mess it up this time. Then I bet they'll notice."

Bearly didn't always have the best ideas. But, Abear was still angry and the more he thought about messing up his clean room, the more he liked the idea.

Abear and Bearly ran back to Abear's cave and tip-toed quietly past Mom and Dad into Abear's room. His parents were hard at work in the kitchen and didn't hear the cubs pass.

"Good-bye clean room," whispered Abear grabbing a paw full of his nicely folded bandannas. They fell like little parachutes as he spun around tossing them into the air.

Bearly had already found some paper to tear into small pieces. "It's snowing," he cried as he scattered the shredded paper.

Toys, books, games and even furniture were tossed about. Finally, they stopped. Sitting in the middle of the room, they couldn't help admiring their mess.

"Time for me to go," said Bearly. He was certain that it wouldn't take long for the <u>messy</u> room to be discovered.

Mom looked up from her work in the kitchen and was surprised to see Bearly leaving. "I didn't know that you were here," she said. Then lowering her voice to a whisper she asked, "Is Abear in his room?"

"Yes ma'am," said Bearly rolling his eyes. "I really need to be going."

"But Bearly," she said, "I want you to see something first."

She led Bearly to the kitchen table. It was filled with Abear's favorite foods.

"Abear worked very hard to clean his room," she said to Bearly. "His father and I are so proud of him that we decided to make his favorite dinner."

Bearly said a quick, polite good-bye and hurried out. He didn't want to know what was going to happen next. As he looked back into the cave he could see Abear walking into the kitchen. He was glad that he wasn't Abear!

Bearly kept thinking, "Did Abear make a mistake? What could he have done differently?"

CHAPTER 6

IT'S MY FISH

Cool water and warm sun, Abear and Weebear loved to go fishing. "We sure haven't had much luck," said Weebear looking down into the fast running water.

"I know," said Abear. "I see plenty of fish, but I just can't catch 'em. Every time I try to scoop one up it runs right out from under my paw."

"At least you can get close to them," said Weebear kicking angrily in the direction of the fish.

Just then the bears saw something floating in the river downstream. It was wide and brown, but they couldn't tell what it was.

"I saw it first," yelled the cubs at the same time. They weren't sure what it was, but a treasure is a treasure. They raced downstream. Being bigger and older, Abear easily beat his little brother to the brown thing in the river.

"It's a net!" shrieked Abear.

"I saw it first! It's mine! It's mine!" shouted Weebear when he finally arrived at the net.

"Is not," claimed Abear holding the net tightly to his chest. Somehow he knew what Weebear would say next.

"I'm telling Mom!" hollered Weebear.

Abear knew that Mom would take the net from both of them if they were fighting over it. "Here," he moaned handing the net to Weebear, "but you won't catch any fish 'cause you don't know how to use it."

Weebear worked and worked with the net. He tried scooping with it. He tried dragging it. He even tied it between his legs and walked upstream. No fish.

Every time he got close to a fish it swiftly swam in the other direction. The fish looked like they were laughing at him.

Abear was laughing too. He knew it would not be long until Weebear gave up. Then it would be his turn. He was certain that <u>he</u> could catch a fish with the net.

Weebear just kept trying. He was determined to catch a fish. Abear began to feel sorry for Weebear. He was so little, and he was trying so hard.

"Here, let me help you," offered Abear.

"No, you can try it by yourself," mumbled Weebear as he threw the net up on the bank. He was tired, wet, and very disappointed.

"Great," said Abear forgetting about Weebear's feelings. "I'll show you how easy it is." Abear grabbed the net and moved into the center of the stream.

Just like Weebear, Abear tried scooping with it. He tried dragging it. Like Weebear he even tied it between his legs and walked upstream. No fish.

The fish swam away from Abear and the net as easily as they had from Weebear. Now it was Weebear's turn to laugh with the fish.

Finally, Abear joined Weebear on the bank. Now there were two disappointed cubs.

No fish in the net. No fish on the bank. No fish in their bellies. Lots of fish in the stream.

"I've got it," said Abear. "You hold the net open, and I'll chase the fish into it."

Weebear thought this was a great idea. Now the bears were really excited. The plan would surely work.

Weebear stretched the net into the water as wide as he could reach. It nearly covered the entire little stream.

Abear moved upstream and began to splash the water as he moved down toward Weebear and the net. The fish weren't laughing now.

One, two, three, four, five fish smashed into the net. Weebear dragged the net filled with fish to the edge of the water.

"Yee haa!" yelled Weebear jumping up and down. "I caught five fish in the net! I did it! I did it! I did it!" Abear couldn't believe what he was hearing.

"You caught them?" he shouted. "I ran them into the net. They're mine."

Weebear grabbed the largest fish out of the net. "They're mine!" he claimed holding the fish close to his furry chest.

Abear grabbed for the big fish and was able to get his paw on the fish's tail before Weebear could yank it away. Abear tugged on the tail, Weebear tugged on the head.

Suddenly the fish popped loose and flipped into the stream. It was gone.

The bears kept tussling with one another even after the fish had escaped. They were so busy arguing and fighting that they didn't see the rest of the fish getting out of the net and flipping back into the river.

"Oh no!" moaned Abear when he noticed the empty net.

Weebear couldn't believe it, "They're gone, they're all gone."

46

The bears felt very silly. They had caught enough fish for both of them, but they had lost them because they wouldn't share.

"There's only one thing to do," said Abear.

"Yep, we'll just have to catch them again," said Weebear.

This time the fish knew about the net and they weren't nearly as easy to catch. Abear would chase the fish and Weebear would hold the net. Then, Weebear would chase the fish and Abear would hold the net.

They stretched the net so many times that it began to rip. Now, most of the fish swam right through the net. Finally, one great big fish, too big to swim through the holes that had ripped into the net, got stuck. The cubs were able to catch this fish, but by the time they got it to the bank the net was completely torn.

Abear and Weebear were very tired, but they held on tightly to the fish. They were about to leave the stream with their prize catch when they saw an old, skinny bear coming down the trail. Having never seen this bear, they watched closely as he entered the stream.

The skinny old bear looked tired and weak as he tried and tried to scoop a fish out of the stream with his paw. He moved too slowly to even come close to the fish. Abear and Bearly knew how hard it was to scoop a fish out of the stream with just your paw.

Finally, the skinny, old bear gave up. He sat in the middle of the stream looking down at the fish that swam all around him.

The cubs felt sorry for the old bear. They could try to help him with the net, but it was all torn. They could try to scoop him a fish with their paws, but they weren't any better than he was. They could give him their fish, but they only had one.

The cubs were very confused. They wondered, "What should we do?"

CHAPTER 7

THE ROPE IS TOO SHORT

Bearette couldn't wait to teach Abear her new card games. She had learned the games from her grandmother and was getting quite good.

Abear was anxious to learn how to play. He loved cards, but he didn't know how to play very many games.

Bearette explained the rules to Abear. He listened carefully. There were a lot of rules and he hoped that he could remember them all.

The first game was not very much fun. Every time Abear tried to do something with his cards, Bearette would cry out, "No Abear, that's against the rules."

He was trying very hard to learn the rules, but it was just too difficult. Finally, Abear had enough, "I quit," he said. "This game's no fun!"

Bearette started to get angry. She thought Abear was quitting because he couldn't win. "Oh, well," she thought, "I'll just teach him another game."

The next game wasn't any easier for Abear to learn. Too many rules. Too many things to remember.

By now, Abear was so confused that he wasn't trying very hard.

"I don't like this game either," he said. "Why can't we play a game that I know?"

They tried to think of a game that they both knew, but they couldn't. Finally, Bearette agreed to learn one of Abear's favorite games.

"This one's easy," said Abear. "There are only a few rules."

Abear told Bearette the rules, but the game didn't sound very easy to Bearette. She decided to give it a try anyway.

Bearette didn't do very well. She kept getting the rules all mixed-up, and Abear kept shouting, "You can't do that!"

It was just like Abear trying to play Bearette's new games. Nothing seemed to be working.

Bearette made so many mistakes, and Abear was yelling so often, that they ended up in a big fight.

Mom heard Bearette and Abear fighting. "What are you two arguing about?" asked Mom. Abear and Bearette began talking at the same time. "Wait, wait," said Mom. "One at a time."

After hearing each cub's story, Mom decided that she should take the cards for a while.

The cubs were very disappointed. They decided to go outside and find something else to do. Once outside they still had trouble deciding on something that would be fun for both of them.

The only things that looked the least bit interesting were two short pieces of rope that they found.

The cubs grabbed the ropes, but neither piece was long enough to be any fun. Abear tried to make a lasso from one piece. Bearette tied the other rope to a tree limb and tried to make a swing. Both bears tried to use their short pieces for a jump rope, but they were just too short!

Then Bearette had an idea. "Let's tie our ropes together and make one jump rope."

"Great idea," said Abear, already tying two ends of the ropes together.

Once tied together, the rope was perfect for jumping. Abear grabbed the rope, and started jumping.

Bearette begged for a turn. Finally, Abear stopped and gave her a chance.

While Bearette was jumping Abear had an idea. "You jump ten times, and then it'll be my turn," he explained.

"Sure," said Bearette. This was a simple rule that they both liked.

Soon, taking turns was easy. Abear would count while Bearette jumped, then Bearette would count while Abear jumped.

The bears were so busy taking turns with the rope that they didn't see Bearly. "Can I have a turn?" asked Bearly as he came walking up the trail.

Abear and Bearette weren't very excited about sharing with Bearly. They had found the ropes. They had tied them together. And, they had thought of the sharing rules.

"We sort of want to play by ourselves," said Bearette.

"Yea, it would be harder to share with three people," added Abear.

Bearly really wanted to jump rope and he had his own plan. Looking around the path, Bearly found another short piece of rope. It was too short to jump, but it would be perfect to add to Abear and Bearette's rope.

It took awhile, but Bearly finally convinced the other cubs to put all of the ropes together and make one long jump rope. Bearly showed them how two of them could hold the ends of the rope and turn it around in big, wide circles while the third cub jumped.

Bearette was first to jump. Abear and Bearly grabbed the ends of the long rope and began to turn it in big circles. Bearette kept jumping until they counted to ten. Then it was Abear's turn. Finally, they counted to ten while Bearly jumped. They were having great fun.

But when it got back to Abear's turn he decided he didn't want to play anymore. He liked holding both ends of the shorter rope and jumping by himself. He didn't want to stop at ten jumps either. "What fun is there in just ten short jumps?" thought Abear.

"I want Bearly to take his rope off," said Abear.

"No," shouted the other two bears.

Now they didn't know what to do. Abear didn't want to play with the long rope. Bearette and Bearly needed Abear to turn the long rope.

Abear needed at least two of the short pieces of rope to be able to jump by himself. None of the bears could think of a good answer. The cubs kept asking themselves, "What should we do?"

CHAPTER 8

WHO'S WATCHING WEEBEAR?

Brown, yellow, and red leaves were piling up outside the bear cave. The air was turning cool and winter was coming soon. Mom and Dad had been gathering food for weeks. Winters were long in this part of bear country, and the bear family would need lots of food.

Mom looked tired when she spoke, "With a little luck we'll have enough food before the snow starts falling."

"I hope we make it," said Dad. He knew that it takes a lot of food for four bears to hibernate through the long winter.

Abear didn't really understand why his parents were so concerned. For him it was just another day and he and Bearly had big plans. They were going to look for shiny rocks at the edge of the forest. He was almost out of the cave when his mother called to him.

"Oh no," he thought, "I know she's going to ask me to watch Weebear."

"It's time for Dad and I to gather more food," said Mom.

Abear knew what was next.

"You know that Weebear has a bad cold and can't go with us. Would you please stay home and take care of him?" she asked.

"Do I have to?" he whined. But it was too late, she had already caught up with Dad as he walked down the trail.

Abear wondered why nothing seemed to be going right. The summer weather had been hot and dry, and now the fall seemed very bad. No rain in the summer meant less food in the fall.

The bears needed lots of food for the long winter. This year there simply wouldn't be enough food. Abear was already hungry and the winter had not even begun. The bears had plenty of food in the spring, but winter would be different.

No one seemed happy. Mom was the saddest. All of her pretty flowers and bushes had died during the dry, hot summer. She loved her flowers. This year they had not bloomed.

Just before he turned to go back into the cave to check on Weebear, Abear spotted Bearly coming up the trail.

"Hey Abear! Let's get going," he shouted, eager to find some shiny rocks.

"I can't," answered Abear. "Weebear has a cold and I have to take care of him."

"Bring him along," said Bearly.

"You can't take a sick little cub out to look for rocks," said Abear frowning. "Besides, he's asleep."

"Sleeping?" replied Bearly. "Great, he won't even know that we're gone."

At first Abear got excited. Then he began to think, "What if Weebear wakes up? What if he needs something? What if Mom and Dad come back?"

"Naa," said Abear, "you better go without me. I need to be here with Weebear."

Now Abear was really unhappy.

Bearly went on his way.

"He'll probably find all of the good rocks," thought Abear as he watched Bearly go down the trail.

Abear didn't want to go back inside the cave. He could hear Weebear if he woke up, and he wanted to enjoy the outdoors as much as he could before it started to snow.

He found a sharp stick and sadly sat in front of the cave drawing little pictures in the sand. He was sad, a little hungry, and very lonely.

"Where's Mom?" asked Abear when he saw Dad coming up the trail alone.

"She's still looking for food," said Dad in a weary voice. He looked tired and worried. Abear knew they must not have found very much food. But, maybe Dad was finished looking for the day. Maybe Dad would be home to watch Weebear.

"Dad," called Abear, "are you going to be around the cave this afternoon?"

Dad didn't answer. He just walked into the cave without looking at Abear. Now Abear didn't know what to do. It looked like Dad would be home for awhile, but he wasn't certain. Surely he would have said something if he were going to leave right away.

The thought of Bearly finding the shiniest rocks was too much for Abear. "Dad must be planning on staying at the cave. Why else would he come back so early?"

Abear suddenly dashed down the trail to find Bearly.

Shortly after Abear left, Dad came out of the cave. He was going back to join Mom to look for food in the woods.

"Abear," he called back into the cave thinking that Abear was still inside, "Mom and I will be back just before dark." By this time Abear was nearly at the edge of the forest.

Bearly, however, wasn't at the edge of the forest. There weren't any shiny rocks there either. Bearly must have already gotten them all. What a horrible year this was turning out to be.

Abear was feeling very sorry for himself -- not much food, no good rocks, and Weebear. Why did he always have to watch Weebear? If it weren't for Weebear and his dumb old cold, he could have gotten rocks with Bearly.

Mom and Dad got back to the cave before Abear. They could hear Weebear crying in the back of the cave. Mom rushed into the cave and found Weebear alone.

She was almost too tired to be angry. Her day had been very long. Looking for food had been difficult, and she hadn't found much.

Mom's year had not been very good either. She started to cry.

When Abear got home Mom was sitting in her rocking chair holding Weebear. Weebear had stopped crying, but Mom still had tears running down her face. She said nothing. She didn't need to say anything. Abear could tell that she was mad, sad, and disappointed.

Dad was upset too. He asked Abear why he left Weebear all alone.

Abear didn't know what to do or say. He couldn't say that it was Dad's fault. He couldn't complain about being tired of watching Weebear -- everyone was tired. He mostly felt badly about his mom. He didn't like to see her un-happy. And, more than anything else he didn't want to disappoint her. He wondered, "What could I have done differently?"

About the Authors

David W. Andrews, Ph.D.

Dr. Dave Andrews has been working with, and studying, children and families for over fifteen years. He has published work on children's friendships, parenting young children, early childhood education, and a variety of other topics. He spent eight years as a university professor, and is currently a researcher at the Oregon Social Learning Center. He also teaches at the University of Oregon and Lane Community College.

Dr. Andrews received training as a psychologist and specialist in child development, obtaining his Ph.D. from Florida State University, M.S. from Kansas State University, and B.A. from Auburn University. He is married, and the father of two daughters.

Lawrence Soberman M.Ed.

Larry Soberman has been involved in education for nearly two decades. He has worked as an elementary school teacher, special educator, counselor, and university instructor. He has also been responsible for developing a number of curricula for parents and children designed to improve child development and parent child relations.

He is currently working as a researcher at the Oregon Social Learning Center where he continues to write and develop programs for children and families. Mr. Soberman obtained his B.S. and M.Ed. in education from the University of Oregon. He will finish his Ph.D. in special education early in 1993, focusing on the role of teachers in helping parents with their children. He is a single parent of two teenage children.

Did You Borrow This Book? Want a Copy of Your Own?

Need a Great Gift?

ORDER FORM

YES, I want to invest $15.95 in my family and have a personal copy of this book. Send _____ copies of Abear for Children and Parents.

Please add $2.00 per book for postage and handling. Allow 30 days for delivery. Send checks payable to: Family Support Systems, P.O. Box 11751 Eugene, OR 97440. Credit card orders may be called to (503) 344-0749

Name _____ Phone (___)_____

Address _____

City _____ State_____ Zip_____

Here is my check or money order for $ _____

Bill my_____ Visa _____ MasterCard Expires_____

Acct. # _____

Signature _____

QUANTITY ORDERS INVITED
For bulk discount prices call (503) 344-0749

ABEAR

FOR PARENTS

David W. Andrews, Ph.D.
Lawrence Soberman, M.Ed.

Illustrated by Ray Yost

Published by Family Support Systems
Eugene, Oregon

Library of Congress Card Number   92-72527

Copies of this book may be ordered from the publisher:

Family Support Systems
P.O. Box 11751
Eugene, Oregon 97440

Parents

Abear is two books in one. The introduction to *Abear for Parents* explains the most effective way to use *Abear for Children*. Please read the Introduction to *Abear for Parents* before reading *Abear for Children*.

Contents

Introduction

About Abear

Abear is a bear -- an ordinary bear with an ordinary family. Abear, his parents, and his little brother, Weebear, are working hard to be a good family. They are learning as they go, the same as any other family. The bears are faced with many choices. Abear must make choices about his friends, family rules, his brother, and many other things. His parents are faced with the monumental task of nurturing their young cubs, guiding them into healthy development.

We all face similar challenges. *Abear* was written to be a fun, informative tool to help you face these challenges. It is not the wonder drug of parenting. It won't help you solve all of the complex problems of being a parent. It will give you something to think about, some specific strategies for dealing with typically difficult situations, and an avenue to talk to your children about important issues.

The information presented is based on simple techniques used by good parents for centuries. The ideas and advice were taken from research on effective parenting and peer relations, thirty years as professionals in child development and education, and our own personal experience. In conducting research on children and families, we have noted two important characteristics of things that *"work"*. First and foremost, they must be fun! Second, they must be simple. *Abear* was designed to be both. Fortunately, fun and simplicity do not limit creativity and innovation. Abear has some unique features that are worth mentioning.

Two books in one with coordinated content for parents and children, is a somewhat novel approach to parent education. One side of this book is titled *Abear for Children*, the other *Abear for Parents*. Their coordinated chapters literally have the effect of putting parents and their children on the *"same page"* in terms of issues. Each chapter of *Abear for Children* presents a real life example

1

(as real as bears can be) of issues faced by parents and children. *Abear for Parents* guides the family through content, discussion, and activities related to the same issue.

Parents and children find common ground in reading *Abear for Children* chapters. Parents are given advice on the issue at hand and strategies for daily living by reading *Abear for Parents*. The result is a coordinated approach that requires the involvement of both parents and children.

Another unique feature is in *Abear for Children*. It is written in a format that uses chapters with open endings. Abear and his family find themselves in some pretty difficult situations, with many questions about what to do next. But, just as in real family life, there are often no easy answers, nor is there one answer that fits every family. Each chapter ends with a dilemma. You and your child must use the story and the information presented in the parent chapter to finish the storyline. There are questions and activities at the end of each parent chapter that will help you do this. It may take children a while to get acquainted with this novel format, but the technique stimulates considerable involvement with the story and the issue being presented.

How to Use Abear

Find a Time and Place   Find one time each week when you, your child(ren), and whomever else is going to participate can look forward to doing Abear. A standard time will help ensure that you get through each chapter. Each chapter, discussion, and activities that follow will take about 45 minutes. Right away Abear is helping you spend this quality time with your child every week. Try to keep the same time and place each week. It is not imperative, but a regular schedule works best. The place should be quiet (no TV) with minimal chances of interruption. You do not need a big space, but the art activities will require some type of flat surface.

One chapter of Abear a week is all that you need. There is parent homework with each chapter that is to be completed each week. Give yourself a full week to do the homework before starting another chapter. If you get behind, or miss a week -- don't worry. Push back your schedule and keep on doing one chapter a week.

Family Involvement   Abear was designed for younger children (preschool through elementary school), but the whole family is invited to participate. It only takes one parent and one child to complete a chapter, but the more the merrier. If the group

swells to an unmanageable size, you may want to set some limits, but it is not required. In fact nothing is absolutely required.

The Parent Book   Each chapter of the parent book starts with a discussion of an issue. *Abear for Children* will portray Abear in a situation that illustrates this issue. You should read the *Abear for Parents* chapter <u>before</u> reading the matching *Abear for Children* chapter with your child.

The Issue   Each chapter begins with a description of an issue related to parenting, and some advice. Eight different issues are presented, one in each chapter. Discipline, communication, making friends, gathering information, dealing with tough situations, sharing and cooperating, setting rules, and stress are all covered. Read about each topic and take the advice into consideration. The information and advice is presented as *"food for thought"*. Every parent will use the information in a slightly different way. Think about each topic and the information presented as it relates to <u>your</u> family.

Storybook Discussion   Each chapter has a section to help facilitate a discussion of the *Abear for Children* chapter. You can use the questions presented in this section to stimulate a discussion of the story with your child. These questions and the following section on artwork will help you complete each storybook chapter with your child, and help resolve Abear's problems. The questions are presented as a starting point for a discussion of *Abear for Children* chapters. Use these questions to get your child(ren) talking about the stories. Feel free to use other questions and let the discussion go in any direction that your child takes it. The idea is to discuss the issue, not to get the right answers to the questions.

Make sure that your child feels free to participate in the discussion. You can do this by praising their ideas, and continuing to prompt them with detailed questions.

Artwork   The art activity is a fun way to continue the discussion and get some closure on *Abear for Children* chapters. The art activity is done when you have discussed each story and come to some agreement on how it should end. You will be drawing a picture of the ending to the story. There are suggestions in each chapter on how and what to draw, but remember the ending of each story is yours. Praise your child for their artwork and make your own contributions to the drawings.

Homework   Yes, you will have weekly homework. Each homework assignment is related to the weekly topic and will give

you an opportunity to practice some of the ideas presented. These are presented as guidelines to help you explore the topic. Try each assignment and use the ones that are helpful.

Reading Abear for Children   Read each chapter of *Abear for Children* to, or with, your child as you would any other children's book. Each story is short and easy to read. If your child is a reader you can decide to read together or take turns. At the end of each chapter ask your child the questions in the corresponding activities section of the *Abear for Parents*. It is a good idea to be familiar with these questions before reading *Abear for Children*.

Keeping it Light

The last thing that any of us need as parents is more work. Abear was not designed to take a lot of time or become a burden to parents. Nor was it created to generate any kind of guilt about what you are doing or not doing as a parent.

Abear has no absolute right and wrong answers. Just as in parenting, some answers and ways of approaching problems are better than others. Use Abear to choose your own answers, those that work best for you and your children. If something is working, keep using it. If it doesn't work, modify your plan or drop it.

Whatever you do keep it light and fun. Parenting is a tough, serious job. Abear is an opportunity to take a lighter look at parenting. Have fun talking about Abear and the sticky situations that he gets into. Enjoy yourselves as you use his problems to take a close look at the way you do things in your own family.

Conclusion

We sincerely believe that since you have read this far you care a great deal about your child's development. Your caring and trying to make *"good"* things happen for your family are your greatest assets. In fact, you are probably already doing many of the things suggested in this book. Keep working on those things and try some of the new ideas. And, most of all, remember to have fun with Abear.

Chapter 1
Communication

From guessing whether a newborn is hungry or wet, to trying to understand teenage slang, communicating with children can be tough. Much of the success and failure of parenthood can be traced to communication. Communication is the heart of good parenting, and most of the issues to be dealt with in future chapters cannot be successfully addressed without it.

Clear communication, established early in children's lives, is the foundation for many other areas of development. Nurturing children into adulthood is nearly impossible without effective communication. Unfortunately, it's not always easy to communicate with children. Communication, in general, is difficult. Many of our conflicts with bosses, spouses, in-laws, or neighbors can be traced to this difficulty.

Communication demands that we play the role of listener one minute and speaker the next. It is difficult to do both, and coordinating when one person speaks and the other listens is even harder. Especially when most of us prefer speaking over listening. It takes at least two people to communicate, each willing to take their turn as listener and speaker.

We become very dependent upon the person that we are communicating with to do their part. The information we send is only as good as the information we receive. It is much like playing catch. You throw the ball and then you catch it. The success of the game depends on good throws and good catches. The game suffers equally from wild throws and missed catches. A listener who misses important information causes as much trouble as a speaker who leaves out important information. One person not doing their part impacts the entire effort to communicate.

If communication in general is difficult, then communication with very young children seems almost impossible. As human

beings, young children are rapidly developing a system of communication that will one day be as complex as any within the animal kingdom. However, during early childhood their language development is not nearly complete and severely limits their ability to communicate.

Preschool children are deceptive in their ability to communicate. They can understand most of what is spoken to them and produce nearly any words they need to express their thoughts. On the surface they look as if they have it all together in terms of communication. However, producing words and understanding phrases are only limited parts of good communication. Granted, they are important parts. But, being a good listener and speaker involves much more. Here are a few pointers.

GOOD LISTENING SKILLS

Pay Attention

Good listeners take the time to hear what is being said. Quietly facing the speaker they make eye contact and listen to every word. They nod their head and use expressions of approval (*"uh-huh"*, *"yes"*, *"I see"*) or disapproval (*"nah-ah"*, *"not really"*, *"I don't think so"*). They don't stare blindly at their shoes as if they lost the penny out of their loafers.

Never Interrupt

Good listeners wait patiently for their turn to speak. They never jump in and finish a sentence for the speaker, or take off on a lengthy speech of their own.

Understand the Speaker's Point of View

Good listeners make a special effort to understand the speaker and their perspective. They think about the issue at hand as the speaker would, putting themselves into the speaker's shoes. They do not try to fit everything that the speaker says into their own thoughts and ideals.

Ask Good Questions

When good listeners are confused or need more information they ask questions to clarify their knowledge. They do not sit quietly acting as if they understand every word when they are not really sure what the speaker means.

GOOD SPEAKING SKILLS

Use Words and Phrases that Listeners Understand

Good speakers are sensitive to their listener's level of understanding and adjust their speech accordingly. They do not talk over the heads of their listeners, using big words to try to impress the listener.

Speak Slowly and Clearly

Good speakers take the time to make themselves clear, pronouncing every word in a way that is easy to understand. They do not mumble incoherently or race through each sentence at the speed of light.

Give Others a Chance to Speak

Good speakers pause every now and then to see if the listener would like a speaking turn. They do not ramble on and on turning blue in the face because they have not paused for a breath.

Check to See If the Listener is Paying Attention

Finally, good speakers look for clues that their listener is paying attention. They check to see if the listener is maintaining eye contact, giving signs that they understand what is being said, or trying to say something.

HELPING CHILDREN LEARN GOOD COMMUNICATION SKILLS

How many children do you know who can consistently meet these standards of good listener or speaker? I would like to claim that my own children meet these standards, but they do not, at least not consistently. While many children are capable, they aren't always motivated or reinforced for good communication skills. There are two ways that parents can help. Parents can help children learn the skills and instill the motivation necessary, or they can adjust their speaking and listening behavior to compensate for the inabilities of their children. I prescribe a little of both.

Our efforts to help children communicate begin with the first day of life. We interpret their needs from their cries. Later, we interpret what they like from the way they point and smile at something special. We shower them with praise for their first spoken word, especially if it's *"ma-ma" or "da-da"*. As they get older

we brag about the number of words that they can chain together to make a sentence.

In a few short years we have nurtured their development to include a wide vocabulary and an unlimited potential for communicating with other people, but they remain miles away from reaching this potential. Sometimes we are so impressed with their development in the first few years that we forget how far they still have to go, and our support begins to dwindle. We often overlook how much we can continue to influence their ability as they move through childhood.

Whether they can't do it, or they just don't, children have a pretty poor reputation as listeners. Failing as a listener has probably led to as many punishing situations for children as any other single behavior. No child will escape their early years without blurting, *"But Mom, I didn't even hear you say that,"* as a first line of defense. However, if you assist your child in practicing the listening skills presented earlier in this chapter they can and will improve.

Helping Little Listeners

Listening Tips *"Pay attention!"* is a phrase used often by parents and teachers. To children it usually means be quiet, sit still, and at least look like you are listening. Parents should always require this as a minimum when speaking to children, especially when conveying important information. Children who are singing along with a cartoon rap video are probably not paying much attention. You should feel comfortable asking a child to give you some evidence of listening. This means turning off the rap cartoon, getting close enough so that shouting is not necessary, and actually maintaining eye contact. Like court subpoenas, face-to-face is the only way to know that the message was received.

Likewise, whenever possible you should model good listening skills for your children by responding to their requests with face-to-face attention. Remember to pay attention, avoid interruptions, try to understand their point of view, and ask good questions.

Too often we are busy, tired, or just uninterested in the story about the turtle who got crushed by the car. Half-hearted listening to their yarns does not set a very good example of good listening. Try asking them to tell you the story at a later time, a time when you are not busy or tired. A time when you might be able to muster up a little interest in the poor turtle.

Interruptions   Interrupting is the only thing more aggravating than not paying attention. You are right in the middle of a sentence when your son starts chanting, *"but, but, but, but...."*. Or better yet, you are in the middle of the same sentence, when your daughter begins to recount a story that happened three weeks ago, and everyone else in the family starts to listen to her. It is often difficult for children to wait their turn to speak. Many times they will interrupt without even realizing that someone else was speaking.

Our first reaction to an interruption is often to compete for the privilege of speaking. Sometimes we simply try to drown out the other person, thinking louder is better. Sometimes we just continue speaking not knowing who is being heard. And, sometimes we simply give in and stop in mid sentence. None of these strategies are useful in teaching children to take turns speaking.

One useful strategy is to let children know when they are interrupting. Give them a signal that reminds them that they are interrupting. Try holding up a hand, as if to say, *"Stop!"* Tell your children that this means stop and wait your turn. It is simple, but amazingly effective. By using a hand signal to stop the interruption you do not have to change what you were saying to respond to the interruption. If this does not stop the interruption you should tell your child that they interrupted, and ask them to wait their turn in the future. Children who continue to interrupt should be asked to leave the conversation for a short period of time until they can return to the conversation without interrupting.

Questions   Most children are born curious. *Enquiring minds want to know.* Sometimes their questions seem unending. Even so, there are times when children will act as if they understand a word, phrase, or concept when they have no idea what is going on. They either assume it is not important, or they are afraid of looking silly by asking a question. My eight-year-old daughter recently wrote a sentence for a spelling assignment in which she stated, *"Last Thanksgiving we had a famine at our house."* Somewhere along the line she interpreted famine as feast. She later admitted that she was not sure of the word's meaning, but was embarrassed to ask for help.

Children should be encouraged to ask questions whenever they are unsure of themselves. They should feel especially comfortable asking questions about things they have heard, but not understood. This is simple to encourage, but requires a tremendous amount of consistency. Children will not ask questions if there is

even a remote chance they will feel stupid for asking it. The old line, *"There is no such thing as a silly question"* does not hold for children. Children will ask some incredibly silly questions. The silliest questions should be responded to with respect and support. Otherwise, children will quickly learn to protect themselves by not asking any questions.

Practice praising good questions. When a child asks a good question they should be praised for the quality of the question before they receive an answer. If Josh asks, *"Mom, could a dinosaur live in our backyard?"* there are at least a hundred different ways to interpret and respond to this question. But, obviously the child is curious, or seriously confused, and would like some information. Regardless of Josh's intent in asking the question, he should be rewarded for trying to get new and improved information. Rather than saying, *"Don't be so silly,"* you might try, *"Well, that's a good question, Josh,"* and then try finding out what in the world he is talking about.

Supporting Speaking Skills

Fast talking gibberish is annoying and hard to understand. Children often need to be reigned in, encouraged to slow down, and prompted to speak clearly. This can be a simple procedure. Without interrupting, give the child a sign that they are going too fast. This works the same as the hand signals for interrupting. You simply want to provide a cue that the speech is too fast and needs to be clear. If this doesn't slow them down, you can politely ask them to start over using a slower tempo and speaking clearly.

Clear speech also means no purposeful baby talk or excessive whining. Baby talk and whining is fine for babies and very young children. Older children, however, need to express themselves without relying on these tricks.

Try to avoid the trap of reinforcing whining and baby talk. These two ways of communicating get your attention and are easy to reward. Parents often reward whining with compassion and baby talk with praise for being cute. Other adults and children don't find it nearly as attractive.

Children who have mastered clear and normal speech will find plenty of opportunities to use it. Hopefully they will use these skills within limits. Sometimes children go for the *Gone with the Wind* version of their stories, rather than sticking to the *Reader's Digest* version. Once on a roll, the details of the most mundane story

just keep on coming. Encourage children to give others a chance to speak. No one appreciates a child, or an adult for that matter, who monopolizes speaking time. Children should be encouraged to speak slowly and clearly, and get to the point.

Children can be guilty of one other communication glitch. They have been known to give speeches to empty rooms. That is, they are not always concerned with who is listening, before they begin talking. *"Mom, I'm going to Megan's to play,"* doesn't communicate much when Mom is not within shouting distance. Likewise, making requests or giving an important message while the listener is on the phone with someone else, listening to music through headphones, or taking a nap is not likely to yield good results. Children can learn to wait to deliver a message until they are sure the listener is tuned in. They simply need encouragement and gentle reminders.

Adjust Behavior and Expectations to Fit the Ability of Children

Adults have a built in thermometer for judging how much a child can handle in terms of giving or receiving information. We simplify our speech for infants, and make it more adult-like for older teens. Sometimes we miss the mark a bit with young children. We either get lazy or simply forget their limitations. Parents can compensate for their child's limitations in communicating by adjusting behavior and changing expectations to match the child's ability level.

Again, it's like playing catch. If you find yourself in a game with a bad catcher you have two options. You can teach the person to be a better catcher, or you can make exceptionally good throws. Parents respond to poor listeners by being exceptional speakers.

There should always be a balance between teaching listening and speaking skills, and compensating for children's limited communication ability. Too much compensation will slow down skill development. Too much of an emphasis on building skills may lead to miscommunication and misunderstanding. Find your own balance as a parent. Teach a little. Compensate a little. Above all be comfortable in talking and listening to your child.

Activities for Chapter 1

After reading the story ask your child the following questions.

1. What did Abear do in the story that he probable should not have done?

Give your child plenty of time to come up with an answer. Ask if there are any other things that Abear could have done differently. If your child seems confused, try to ask the question a different way. "What did Abear do that bothered his mom?" Help your child recognize that:
   a. Abear did not understand the word "seldom".
   b. Abear may not have been listening to everything that his mother was saying.
   c. Abear used a word that he was not sure he understood.
   d. Abear misled Bearly's mom.

Praise any attempts to describe Abear's actions. The idea is to generate a discussion of Abear's communication problems. Try to get information about your child's perspective of that problem. Add your own thoughts about Abear's behavior.

2. What could Abear do next time?

How might Abear avoid these kinds of situations? What could he do the next time he does not understand something? Give your child time to come up with ideas and then point out the following:
   a. Abear could have told Mom he liked the sound of the word seldom but that he really did not know its meaning.
   b. Abear could have used another word when talking to Bearly's mom.
   c. Abear could have practiced using the word "seldom" with his mom or dad.

3. What could Mom have done differently?

Remember that parents need to pay close attention to their children's ability to understand. Parents need to adapt their speech to the listening skills of their child. Give your child an opportunity

to talk about what Mom might have done differently when talking to Abear. Point out the following:

    a. Mom could have chosen a word that she was sure Abear understood.

    b. Mom could have seen that Abear was not sure of the meaning of "seldom", and explained its meaning.

    c. Mom could have asked Abear if he knew the meaning of "seldom".

4. What should Abear and his mom do with the food? What should happen to Abear for causing the misunderstanding? What should they tell Bearly and his mom? What should Abear and his mom do to make sure this kind of misunderstanding does not happen again?

Art Activity

Draw a picture of what happens after Abear tells his mom what he had said to Bearly's mom about the food. Follow one of these options:

    a. You and your child can draw a picture together.

    b. You and your child can draw your own pictures and then compare them.

Whether you draw a picture together or separately be sure to keep an ongoing discussion of the things being drawn. Have your child tell the end of the story using the picture that was drawn.

Parent Homework

You are the best judge of your child's communication strengths and weaknesses. In this section you will be asked to use this knowledge to help develop your child's communication skills.

Step 1   Choose an area that you think would be most helpful to your child's communication development. This skill can be a listening or speaking skill described in the section Helping Children Learn Good Communication Skills. *Example: Speaking slowly and clearly.*

Step 2   Reread the section on the skill you have selected and note the suggestions made.

Step 3   Choose a specific time each day to communicate with your child and practice the skill you have selected. This can be as short as five or ten minutes daily. Make sure it is a time when you are not busy with other tasks so you can give your full attention. It is important that you choose a time when there are plenty of opportunities to practice the skill. When you notice the skill being used correctly reward your child with attention or praise. If possible (without embarrassing) correct your child when you see the selected skill misued.
Example: If you are working on speaking slowly and clearly, choose a time when your child is likely to have something to say. This may be at mealtime, after school, or during a special time set aside for talking.
Praise slow and clear speech and remind your child to slow down when speaking too fast.

Step 4   When you notice your child using the selected skill with you and other people, at home and in other settings, continue praising these efforts. Then, select a new skill to help your child develop other areas of communication.

Chapter 2
Discipline

If communication is the heart of good parenting then discipline is surely the soul. While most agree that "discipline" is important, few agree on what good discipline involves. Discipline means different things to different people. Many definitions of discipline are very narrow and limiting. Some think of discipline as punishment, or a way to control an annoying behavior. There are, however, much broader definitions of discipline, ones that can be very useful in facing the tough situations of parenthood.

Discipline comes from the Latin word *disciplina* which means training. Training involves considerably more than punishment. To train is to shape and encourage the positive, as well as trying to eliminate the negative. This broad definition of discipline is very useful when dealing with the responsibilities of being a parent. Children are pupils and parents are responsible for their training. To discipline is to train the skills necessary in growing up successfully. By this broad definition, what else could be more important to you as a parent than good discipline.

It is helpful to think of discipline as a training system that is designed to help children become self-sufficient, happy, and productive adults. Anything that you do as a parent to assist your child in achieving these goals is part of this system of discipline.

Wow! What a chore. On the surface it seems like too much to handle, but it's not. There are two simple characteristics of a good discipline system: comprehensiveness and consistency. If you can develop a comprehensive approach to discipline that is at the same time consistent, you have put yourself into a position to be successful.

COMPREHENSIVE DISCIPLINE

A comprehensive system of discipline means that it is designed to handle nearly any situation in which learning takes place.

Remember, good systems of discipline are not designed for the exclusive purpose of correcting children who are misbehaving. Good discipline is much more than good punishment.

Learning Environments

Creating a learning environment is the first step toward comprehensive discipline. Learning includes distinguishing right from wrong, developing ways to achieve goals, finding out what is safe and what is not safe, and many other lessons about life. Creating an environment where all of these types of learning can take place requires thinking ahead.

Purposefully setting the stage for learning takes forethought. It means: a) establishing goals and expectations, b) maintaining situations that make these goals easy to attain, and c) listing the ground rules. These are the origins of a sound, comprehensive approach to discipline.

Goals and Expectations Establishing specific goals and expectations is critical. Many of the goals that we set for our children are too vague to be of any real value. Most parents want their children to be *"good"*, but what does that mean? Does it mean that they should always eat their spinach, or that they shouldn't set fire to grandmother's sofa? Unclear goals and expectations do very little to help create productive learning environments.

Creating clearer goals is not always difficult. This can usually be accomplished by addressing the three W's. **What** are the behaviors, and **When** and **Where** should they occur?

Bedtime often requires skillful discipline. It seems to be a time when children are particularly good at finding the loopholes in what you expect of them. How do you accomplish a general goal of training children to ready themselves for bed? I can attest that with young children, "Please get ready for bed," is futile.

But specifying: "**What** I want you to do is put on your pajamas, and **Where** I want you to do this in your bedroom, and **When** I want you to do this is before the big hand gets on the six," is more likely to produce the desired results.

There are two reasons that unclear goals or expectations don't work. First, children don't really know what you want. And, when you haven't been clear, it's easier for them to claim that they didn't know what you wanted them to do. *"Oh, I didn't know that you wanted me to put on my pajamas, you just said get ready for bed."*

16

Maintaining Learning Environments   The second necessity in creating learning environments is to maintain situations that promote the behaviors that you want to see. If a child tries to get ready for bed and finds a bedroom occupied by another sleeping child, missing pajamas, and the big hand already close to the six, the chances of the child accomplishing your bedtime goals are minimal. However, if pajamas and a bedroom are easy to find and there is plenty of time, the child is likely to accomplish the goal. If it is impossible to set up a situation in such a way that leads to success in achieving the goal, smaller more realistic goals should be considered.

Establishing Ground Rules   Finally, it is essential when creating comprehensive discipline systems that you consider the "ground rules" for the specific situation. Consider all of the exceptions, special conditions, and rare possibilities that may arise when children set out to achieve goals.

It is similar to the beginning of a baseball or softball game when the umpire meets with both teams to discuss the ground rules. The umpire carefully goes over the *"what ifs"* that need to be considered. What if a home run ball bounces off of the peanut vendor and lands in the glove of the left fielder. Anticipating these bizarre events is necessary in a comprehensive discipline system.

Suppose you have a goal that your four-year-old child play quietly in her room during rest time. What should she do if she needs to throw up? What if she just wants a glass of water? What if she just wants a book? What if she just wants to talk to you? What if she just wants to come out and walk around? The true question is where are the boundaries, and are there any exceptions? What are the ground rules?

Anticipation is important in establishing ground rules. Children are predictably unpredictable. Young children will actively seek the loopholes in your system. This can work for and against your best training efforts. It works for you in that you know ahead of time that you need to explore all possibilities in establishing the ground rules. It is likely that a five-year-old child who has been asked to clean a bedroom will stuff everything that is not tied down into the closet. So, one ground rule associated with cleaning the bedroom should be no stuffing of things into the closet.

On the other hand, it is impossible to anticipate every ground rule. Even the big league umps miss a few, but they still

meet before every game to talk about events that they are able to anticipate.

CONSISTENT DISCIPLINE

It's simple, consistency works. Once you have developed a system of discipline, consistently helping children achieve specific goals becomes critical. This is accomplished by selectively rewarding attempts to achieve the goals, while ignoring or punishing those behaviors that are incompatible with the goals. The consequences of meeting or not meeting parental expectations should be clearly and consistently administered.

Many children aggrevate their parents by responding to every question with a muffled *"uh-huh"*. Suppose you decide to set a goal of getting a clear *"yes"* as an answer to a question. Most children can slip a dozen or so *"uh-huhs"* past you before you notice it and eventually require a firm "yes".

Inconsistency in rewarding *"yes"*, and failing to correct the *"uh-huhs"*, has created many children who are comfortable mumbling their way through most conversations. But there's good news and there's bad news.

The good news is consistency works. Setting reasonable goals and helping children consistently achieve these goals is the core of good discipline.

Here's the bad news. Total consistency is almost impossible to achieve. Life's unique circumstances constantly interfere with consistent discipline. Fatigue, public places, stress, relatives, our forgetfulness, and a host of other factors contribute to how consistently and appropriately we reward and punish our children.

Consistency is also affected by our inability to constantly monitor the behavior of our children. As children get older they spend less time in front of their parents. It is difficult to consistently discipline children when you are not aware of exactly what they are doing or not doing. The less able you are to observe the behavior of children, the less likely you are to be able to respond to behaviors that are compatible or incompatible with specific goals.

If the general rule is consistency is better, and the general practice is such that you can't be consistent, why bother? Well, before wringing your hands and crying "help", consider this. It is better to change or modify goals or rules rather than to be inconsistent.

Goals as Rules

Often, though not always, goals are stated as rules that govern behavior. For the sake of demonstrating the importance of consistency it is useful to talk about rules as a specific type of goal. A rule that's not consistently enforced probably shouldn't be a rule. Why have rules that aren't enforceable?

Take a lesson from the 55 MPH speed limit -- a good rule that wasn't consistently enforced. The answer? Return to 65 MPH, a more enforceable limit. It's easier to start with guidelines you are both willing and able to enforce.

What about a rule requiring sleep at nap time? Nothing short of a strong sedative can make a child (of any age) sleep on command. Children can be made to lie down in their beds for specific periods of time, and most young children will end up asleep. But, a rule requiring sleep is destined for failure or modification. Evaluate the feasibility of a rule before it becomes a law.

Exceptions to the Rules Exceptions to the rules should be clearly identified. Tell children, of all ages, when the rules are in effect and when they are not. In situations where there is clearly no way to enforce the rules, or in situations where the rules aren't appropriate, inform children <u>before</u> they test the limits.

For example, picnics elicit some of the worst table manners from children and adults alike. Many families overlook normal rules of etiquette during these outings. Using your fingers, reaching across the table, eating while standing, and even spitting seeds become acceptable behaviors. Most parents communicate to children, either formally or informally, that in this special situation called "picnic" different rules are in effect.

The same logic should extend to other situations where the normal "law" is temporarily suspended. Children constantly test rules for ambiguity. They are compelled to find out: *Is it a rule or a suggestion?* Recognizing and explaining situations in which the rules are not going to be enforced reduces confusion. It is simple enough to say, *"Right now that behavior is O.K., but as soon as we get back home the house rules stand."*

Monitoring Rules Rules or goals that require behaviors that are hard to monitor will also be hard to enforce. Perhaps you have a goal of helping your child learn to share with other children. And perhaps your child plays with other children mostly at daycare,

while you are working. How can you reinforce or punish behaviors that help your child achieve the goal? You probably need to get help from the teacher (she/he would become your "enforcer" in the school setting) or you need to modify your expectations.

Flexibility and Rules   The quickest way to get into trouble is to carve into stone your most current rules (and goals) as if they will last forever. Forever is a long time. Kids get older. Parents get older. What's "in" changes. What's "out" changes. Parents are faced with the challenge of sticking to their guns, yet being responsive to change. Knowing when a rule has outlived its usefulness is another key to successful discipline.

Changing, eliminating, or updating rules is not admitting defeat. Such modifications are always necessary when teaching standards of conduct. Unchangeable rules die a slow, hard death and can lead to conflicts with your child. Daylight savings time has ruined many eight-o-clock bedtimes. What self-respecting seven-year-old wants to go to bed in broad daylight? Changing bedtime may be much more effective than trying to enforce a rule that only works in the winter.

Demonstrating the importance of updating rules and regulations teaches children some valuable lessons that go beyond effective discipline. Replacing rules no longer necessary can demonstrate new confidence in children. Substituting *"You only cross the street with an adult,"* with *"Be careful and remember to look both ways,"* demonstrates new faith and confidence.

Children also learn that rules have reasons. We all occasionally need help in seeing the relevance of certain rules. Rules are much more likely to be perceived as necessary when there is evidence that they are only going to be rules as long as they are serving a purpose. Communicate the purpose of rules from their inception until their termination.

Conclusion

Don't be afraid to experiment with different systems of discipline, and above all, be the first to admit when a plan is not working. Why jeopardize an entire system of discipline for one unenforceable rule or one unattainable goal? Parenting is a lifelong process. We're in it for the duration. Anticipate the requirements of your discipline system and choose your battles wisely.

Activities for Chapter 2

After reading the story ask your child the following questions:

1. What things did Abear do that he probably should not have done or should have done differently?

    You should give your child plenty of time to come up with answers without help. Try different ways of asking the questions if he/she cannot answer. You might try asking, "What did Abear do wrong?" or, "What are some of the bad things that Abear did?" or, "What do you think that Abear did that his parents will be angry about?" However, younger children may need some prompting. You might try going back to the story and showing the pictures. There are at least five things that could be pointed out.

    a. Abear didn't tell Dad the truth about what Mom had said.
    b. Abear went too close to the falls.
    c. Abear climbed down the falls.
    d. Abear let Bearly talk him into going down the falls.
    e. Abear didn't get home until after dark.

    Let your child talk about any of Abear's behavior. You might even ask what was the "worst thing" that he did. In talking about these behaviors make an effort to get your child to explain why each action was wrong. You may be surprised at the reasoning. You, as a parent, should discuss your own ideas about what was wrong to do and which were the "worst" violations of the rules. If it really bothered you that Abear told a lie, let this be known. If letting Bearly influence his decision about climbing the cliff is disturbing to you, tell your child. Or, if, in the same situation you would be most concerned about safety, let your child hear about it. The idea is to let the story elicit a discussion of your own family values.

2. What could Abear do next time?

    In this question you should try to help your child find creative and acceptable solutions to the problem of wanting to go fishing. If your child has trouble coming up with anything you might suggest the following.

    a. Abear could have told Dad that Mom had never let him go fishing alone, but that he thought he was old enough.
    b. Abear could have asked Dad to take him fishing.

c. Abear could have turned around at the top of the cliff and come home. The next day he would have known the right way to get to the cliff.
d. When Abear got to the fork in the road, he might have gone back to the cave and asked Dad which way to go.

3. What did Dad do that he could have done differently?

Again, let your child come up with ideas. But, you might think about bringing up the following:
   a. Dad could have waited and asked Mom whether or not she let the cubs go alone.
   b. Dad could have decided on his own that he didn't want the cubs going. He could have explained that Mom has rules when she is home and that his rules may be a little different. If he really thought that it was dangerous for the cubs to go alone to the waterfall, he could have explained his concerns.
   c. Dad could have offered to walk the cubs to the waterfall.
   d. Dad could have been more clear about climbing up or down the waterfall.

4. Should Abear be punished? What specifically should he be punished for? For lying? For going to the falls alone? For climbing down? For getting wet? For coming home after dark? What should his punishment be?

Art Activity

Draw a picture of what happens after Abear tells his parents about his day. Follow one of these options:
   a. You and your child can draw a picture together.
   b. You and your child can draw your own pictures and then compare them.

Whether you draw a picture together or separately be sure to keep an ongoing discussion of the things being drawn. Have your child tell the end of the story using the picture(s) that was drawn.

Parent Homework

Your homework is to start experimenting with discipline as a way to change behavior. Most of you will have lots of experience in this area, but practice makes perfect. Follow the steps below.

Step 1 Select a behavior that you would like to see changed in your child. Use the following guidelines in selecting the behavior that you want to work on.

    a. Pick a behavior that is important for you to change. If this is a behavior that you really want to change you are more likely to stick with a plan to change it.

    b. Pick a behavior that happens daily, something that you would like to see happen, or not happen, on a daily basis. Things like chores, school homework, fighting with brothers and sisters, etc.

    c. Pick something that you can consistently keep up with and reward. Sharing with friends at school would be a poor choice unless you accompany your child to school and observe sharing.

    d. Pick a single behavior that will be easy for your child to achieve. One small improvement is all you are looking for. This exercise is designed for practice and confidence, not to develop perfect angels.

Step 2 Find a small reward that can be given daily when the behavior is demonstrated. The important word here is small. Anything that is a little different from the everyday treat will work. Stickers are great. Little stars drawn neatly on a piece of paper are also good. If you want to be a little more elaborate in rewarding your child feel free, but keep it small.

Step 3 Develop a way of keeping track of daily progress on changing the behavior. The best strategy is to develop a chart (an example is given on the next page) and put it in a very visible place -- maybe on the refrigerator. If you don't like the form you might think about a jar with marbles or dried beans to help keep track of days your child did well on the goal. You simply need to know how many days the behavior was good enough to receive the reward, and whether or not you gave the reward.

Behavior to change:

Day of Week	Did the behavior happen?	Was the behavior rewarded?
Monday		
Tuesday		
Wednesday		
Thursday		
Friday		
Saturday		
Sunday		

Chapter 3
Friends

One of the most disheartening times of parenthood is the day your child comes home convinced they have no friends. Whether it's true or not, you can't stand thinking that your *"baby"* feels friendless. You are certain your child is one of the cutest, brightest, funniest and most compassionate kids around. Any other kid with an ounce of sense would be honored to share their company.

Friends Are Important

We understand, as parents, the importance of social interaction and friendship, and most of us are anxious to enhance this area of development in our children. The importance of early friendships for children is also well documented in research about children and their development.

Many of the problems that children experience later in life, especially during the teenage years, can be traced to early problems with being accepted by other children. For example, young children without adequate friendships are more likely to become juvenile delinquents, use and abuse drugs, suffer from depression, and drop out of school.

Parental concern over the social relationships of their children is well justified. This concern is even more justified when considering the stability of early peer relations. Children who are not well liked when they are young, are very likely to be not well liked as adults. If no one likes you when you are five, chances are no one will like you when you are twenty-five, thirty-five, or sixty-five. Many young children who have substantial problems making friends never learn how to develop and maintain relationships.

Making and maintaining friends is a challenging task and can be hard work for even the most skilled child, or for that matter

the most skilled adult. Yet, sometimes we underestimate the complexity of social relations, and assume that we do not need to pay any special attention to helping children establish friendships. Young children are just beginning to develop the skills that will lead to healthy adult relationships, and there are many things that parents (and teachers) can do to stimulate a child's social development.

A critical period of time to focus on social development is during early childhood (preschool through the third grade). This is a period of trial and error in the development of social skills. Prior to the preschool years the most significant relationships in a child's life have been with their parents and their siblings. Suddenly, during the preschool years, children find themselves sharing more and more time with other children their same age. These *"peers"* play a new and significant role in children's development.

First Friendships

Interaction with adults or siblings is not the same as interaction with peers. Adults and siblings are not *"equal"* to children when they interact. Consequently, there are rules of interaction between young children and adults (or older siblings) that do not apply to interactions between young children and their peers. Adults have certain privileges in interacting with children. They often dominate interactions by directing children to perform certain acts, *"Tell your mother what we saw at the pet store."* Or by leading them through the interaction with a series of questions, *"Why don't we talk about what you did at school today?"*

Interactions with same-aged peers are much less structured because of the equality of the children participating. Children who are approximately the same age have roughly the same social ability and are not governed by the same rules that apply to adult-child relations. If one child suggests playing tag, and the other child wants to play hide-and-go-seek, there is likely to be some sort of negotiation before a game is decided upon. There may be similar negotiations between adults and children, but in adult-child relations there is always the threat of the adult making the final decision.

Children are also more motivated to *"stay in good standing"* with their friends than they are with their parents. Kids are stuck with their parents. If children make their parents angry, they are not putting the longevity of the relationship with their parents at

risk. Parents can't proclaim, *"You won't share, so you're not my kid anymore."* On the other hand, children's relationships with peers are not very permanent and can be terminated with a similar proclamation, *"You won't share, so you're not my friend anymore."*

Friends Through a Child's Eyes

Another major difference between adult and child social relationships is the way they perceive their friendships. What it means to be a "friend" changes considerably from childhood to adulthood. In fact, there are several stages that children go through before developing their adult concept of what it means to be someone's friend. Robert Selman, a specialist in children's friendships, outlined four stages that characterize the development of our concepts of friendship.

Stage One　In the first stage (prior to elementary school) young children define their friendships based on proximity. Friends are children to whom they have access. Neighbors, children attending the same preschool, relatives, and others with whom they may have contact during a typical day are the most likely candidates to be labeled as a friend.

If a three-year-old is asked to name a best friend, it is likely to be the child that they are around the most. Furthermore, if asked why this child is their friend, they will explain that they are friends because of the contact they have with one another, *"Shes in my school,"* or *"We play outside together."* In the child's mind they are friends because they spend time together. Obviously, by the time children get to be adults they have redefined friendship. As adults, our neighbors or our office mates are not necessarily our closest friends. Adults are more likely to claim that they spend time with another person because they are friends, not vice-versa.

Stage 2　In Stage 2 older children (kindergarten through second grade) are more likely to attribute friendship to the things that other children do for them. *"Joey is my friend because he let me play with his new toy,"* or *"Megan is my friend because she helped me clean my desk."* This stage has been labeled *"one-way assistance."* Children this age tend to define relationships based on what they are able to get out of them. I have noticed that my six-year-old daughter's popularity during the summer months is partially based upon how many popsicles are left in the freezer, and how willing I am to let her distribute them to the neighborhood gang.

Stage 3   Children in middle childhood (second through sixth grade) are more likely to define friendship based on *"fair-weather cooperation."* They will often say, *"Jordan and I are best friends. I helped him do his homework, and he taught me a new card game."* Children this age cooperate with one another, but only as long as it is clear that everyone is getting something out of the interaction. This type of friendship ends as soon as one person decides that it is no longer beneficial to them.

Stage 4   Most children do not develop a concept of friendship that is consistent with adult thinking until sometime after they are 11 or 12 years old. At this time, they begin to define relationships based on more internal characteristics of themselves and their friends. At this stage they may say, *"We have a lot in common,"* or *"My friend understands me,"* or *"We can always depend upon one another."* This more advanced notion of friendship leads to more permanent relationships.

Children's early notions about the meaning of friends are important for parents to recognize. Otherwise, you might think about your children's peer relations using adult values and definitions of friendship. This can lead to a misinterpretation of the relationship between two children.

Helping Children with Friendships

There are many ways that parents can help children develop healthy relations by taking advantage of the way children think about friendship. Understanding that the nature of children's friendships is changing very quickly is the first step in helping them grow in their social relations.

Three and Four-Year-Olds   Friendships among three and four-year-old children form quickly and dissolve quickly. You can maintain friendships during this age period quite easily. Maintain proximity between children and you can maintain the relationship. A parent who provides opportunities for children to play with a particular group of children is in a sense creating friendships with other children.

But, you should not be overly concerned when children this age break down in tears and shout, *"Claire said I'm not her friend anymore."* Chances are that your child will be back on Claire's best friend list before you can decide how to react.

There is one trap associated with children who equate friendship with proximity. The ability to end a relationship by

moving to a different part of the room allows children to escape from conflict without learning to resolve problems. The simple notion, *"If I'm playing with you, then I'm your friend,"* and, *"If I'm not playing with you, I'm not your friend,"* allows children to move in and out of relationships without a good understanding of how to get along with each other. A child who does not like the rules of a particular game can simply move on to something else and leave both the game and their relationships behind.

You are faced with the task of finding situations that stimulate children's desire to stay with peers for longer periods of time, even when the child may want to move on to other relationships because of a conflict that is interfering with their current friendship. Parents and teachers often overlook the importance of making children work out their differences and come to a successful joint resolution of a problem. I have witnessed many new teachers separating children who have gotten into a squabble. They often physically place such children in opposing corners of the room. When *"separation"* is used as a way of dealing with conflicts between children we are in essence saying, *"If you two cannot play together, I'm not going to let you play together."*

The only way that children are going to progress in their interpersonal relationships is to practice, and this is an area of development where it is impossible to practice by oneself. Therefore, separating children who need to be working out their differences denies these children the opportunity to practice.

A better approach is to sit with children who are fighting over a toy and help them work out a system for taking turns. Don't allow the children to escape to the comfort of another relationship. Remember, there is usually another child waiting on the other side of the room to *"become a friend."* Children should be encouraged to resolve the basic conflict before being encouraged to move on to other relationships.

Children will learn valuable skills about getting along with others, and will also begin to realize that it takes a little work to stay *"close"* within a relationship. If adults thought like three and four-year-olds, we wouldn't need divorce. You could simply retreat to the bathroom, kitchen, or backyard and terminate the marriage until you were ready to begin anew with your spouse.

Five, Six, and Seven-Year-Olds Five, six, and seven-year-olds will demand proximity and more from their friends. These children will likely define their friendships based upon *"What's in*

it for me?" As children get older the importance of sharing resources amplifies. Time, toys, food, and other resources are likely to play a role in the identification of friends. A friend is someone who gave you one of their cookies at lunch. A friend helped you find your bracelet that you lost on the playground.

Parents with children this age need to be sensitive about more than proximity. Now, it's not enough to simply provide the opportunity for children to interact. Now, some attention needs to be paid to the things that go on between children when they are together. Children this age are most successful when they offer something to the relationship, not when they are first to demand something. These offerings can be tangible, like sharing a toy, or bringing something extra to the snack table. Or, they can be less tangible, like helping with a special piece of artwork or finding a lost library book.

Even though friendships in five, six and seven-year-olds are based on more than proximity, they are often relatively short-lived relationships. It is not unusual for my six-year-old to reorganize her list of *"best friends"* frequently. Most of her stable friends stay somewhere near the top of the list, but the order can change dramatically. It is almost impossible to keep up with the rankings. However, the reasons for picking the *"best friend for the day"* are consistent. The child most likely to be nominated is the one who has most recently given her something or done something nice for her. It appears to be based on the slogan, *"What have you done for me lately?"*

Parents can help children this age in several ways. One obvious thing is to make sure your child has something to contribute to new relationships. It is sad to think that you can buy your way into a relationship, but it's true. Remember, both tangible and intangible *"gifts"* are accepted. Teaching children to share and be helpful is essential to their ability to establish relationships with other children.

However, there is one small catch. Young children are not particularly good at sharing and being helpful to one another. Remember, children this age are into the relationship based on what it offers to them, not what they can offer to the relationship. They get so busy looking for what is in it for them, that they forget about contributing something to the relationship. To expect children under eight or nine years of age to consistently deny their own self-interests to ensure the best interests of their friends should be

encouraged, but is not totally realistic. More information on this topic is presented in a discussion of egocentrism in Chapter 6.

Eventually most children see the benefits of giving first, and asking for something out of the relationship second. Unfortunately, we all know people who do not seem to have matured to that level. It's never too early to start promoting these helping and supportive behaviors in children. They may not fully understand the value of these behaviors, and they may not always demonstrate them to the degree that we would like, but practice makes perfect.

Eight-Year-Olds and Up Older children's friendships are starting to look much more like adult friendships. Nine-year-olds cooperate well with one another, get involved in more permanent relationships, and can tell you that their friends mean more to them than what types of goodies they have. However, these relationships are still relatively fragile. Squabbles are common among friends. And, only the closest friendships are not susceptible to daily shifts in rank.

Children this age also need unstructured time with friends. Time to solve important problems; like when to go to the mall; which movie to see; how to deal with new interest in the opposite sex; and many other things that might seem trivial to parents. You should be looking for some stability in your children's friendships, but don't be surprised if there is still a revolving door of friends with a few new faces regularly.

Conclusions

Given what researchers have learned about children and their relationships with their peers, three specific recommendations emerge.

Practice Makes Perfect Improving social relationships requires practice, practice, and more practice. The opportunities for social interaction will increase with the amount of practice that a child gets. Once they begin to develop social skills, other children will seek them out for more interactions, thus more practice.

Parents are the Best Model for Children to Follow Interacting with a wide range of adults in the presence of children, and showing them how to cooperate during these interactions is very helpful. It is also beneficial to demonstrate cooperation within your interactions with your children. If you are always the director and have to be in complete charge of all activities, your child is likely to play the same role in his or her relationships with other children.

Improving Relationships with Others Involves Trial and Error

There will be disappointing times that parents will experience with their children. Times when children think that no one likes them; times when they think that they are being left out by the crowd; and times when they feel betrayed by a friend. Each of these situations provide invaluable experience for children and should not be interpreted as social failures. Parents should encourage children to solve social problems one at a time, and continue on with their relationships. I have heard parents encourage children to dissolve relationships over a conflict. I've heard them say, "*Well just don't ever play with her again.*" This is a mistake. Children should practice resolving conflicts and should be encouraged to work through minor problems with friends before considering giving up and finding new relationships.

One thing that is clear, without the opportunity to interact, children are not likely to develop into socially competent adults. Parents should make every opportunity to encourage social interactions in their children with a wide variety of children and adults. This is a specific area of development where nothing beats experience.

Activities for Chapter 3

After reading the story ask your child the following questions.

1. What did Abear do in the story that he might have done differently?

Give your child plenty of time to come up with an answer. Ask if there are any other things that Abear could have done differently. If your child seems confused, try to ask the question a different way. "What did Abear do that caused the problem with his friends?" Help your child recognize that:

    a. Abear wanted to meet a new friend.
    b. Abear forgot that he was headed to Bearly's house.
    c. Abear did not include Bearly in the fun with the stilts.
    d. Abear did not apologize for hurting Bearly's feelings.

Praise any attempts to describe Abear's actions. The idea is to generate a discussion of Abear's problems with his friends. Try to get information from your child about his or her perspective of that problem. Add your own thoughts about Abear's behavior.

2. What could Abear do next time?

How might Abear avoid this kind of situation? What could he do the next time he has two friends he wants to play with? Give your child time to come up with ideas and then point out the following:

    a. Abear could have explained to Bearette that he needed to go to Bearly's house before he could play with her.

    b. Abear could have introduced Bearette to Bearly and included him in the fun.

    c. Abear could have explained to Bearly why he stopped to play with Bearette.

    d. Abear could have asked Bearly and Bearette what they wanted to do so they could have decided together.

3. What could Bearly and Bearette have done differently?

    a. Bearette could have introduced herself to Bearly and given him a turn with the stilts.

    b. Bearly could have told Abear that he was angry that Abear had not come to his house.

    c. Bearly and Bearette could have included Abear in their game of marbles.

    d. Bearly and Bearette could have decided together with Abear which game to play.

4. What should Abear do? Should Abear ask for another turn? Should he suggest that they all go to the river? Should he tell Bearly and Bearette how angry and confused he is feeling? Or, should he go home and find something else to do?

Art Activity

Draw a picture of what happens after Abear has his turn with the marbles. Follow one of these options:

    a. You and your child can draw a picture together.

    b. You and your child can draw your own pictures and then compare them.

Whether you draw a picture together or separately be sure to keep an ongoing discussion of the things being drawn. Have your child tell the end of the story using the picture that was drawn.

Parent Homework

Getting involved with your child's friendships can be tricky. Children, for the most part, need to work out their own problems with their friends. Most of what you can do as a parent involves understanding their friendships and supporting their efforts to make good friendships.

Step 1   Get information about your child's friendships. There are two ways to get this information. First, you can ask your child about friends (Who do you play with the most? Who is your best friend? Do you think you have good friends?). Or, you can observe your child at play with friends. Remember, friendships that change often are not necessarily a problem, in fact the more friends the better. Use this information to decide whether you want to focus on making opportunities for your child to interact with more friends (Step 2) and/or on helping your child with specific friendships (Step 3).

Step 2   Think of two ways you can increase the opportunities for your child to make new friends. You might consider taking your child and a new friend bowling, skating, or to the movies. Or, get your child involved in an after school activity where there are new friends to make. Try to think of activities where the children have plenty of opportunities to interact. Think about the types of kids you want your child to meet and choose activities where they are likely to be.

Step 3   Model good friendship making skills and praise your child's efforts to make new friends. If your child brings friendship problems to you, take time to listen. Be understanding, even if the problem seems trivial.

Chapter 4
Tough Situations

Why are supermarkets such a haven for misbehaving children? Is it because aisles are designed like mini-dragstrips with breakable wall boundaries, and children are given a metal cart with one bad wheel that makes it hard to push in a straight line? Or because store owners, with plenty of marketing savvy, place the Frosted Flakes with the *free prize in every box* at eye level to a five-year-old?

More parents are angered, embarrassed, and frustrated by the behavior of their children in supermarkets than in most other settings. When parent and young child enter the supermarket, odds are one will exit in tears or tantrum.

Supermarkets are a temptation for young children. But, so are kitchen cabinets, the shelves in the garage, mom or dad's office, and their brother or sister's room. So, why do children show off behaviors in the supermarket that they would never exhibit at home? Why would a four-year-old pop the tops on a six pack of soda at the local market, when at home he wouldn't draw a cup of water from the faucet without permission?

The problem is not in the design of supermarket aisles, nor in the strategic location of the best cereal prizes. Children have a tendency to become out of control in the supermarket just as they do in a variety of other settings outside of their own home. Why? There are two different, but related explanations.

It Works Best at Home

First, as parents we develop an arsenal of strategies to control children's behavior, refining these strategies until they are somewhat successful. Unfortunately, the majority of these strategies work best in the privacy of our home. Along with rewarding children's *"good"* behavior we often resort to some combination of scolding, gentle squeezing, and suppressing privileges as a means of helping children manage their behavior. Most parents are not comfortable using these discipline techniques in public. We are

often very self-conscious about dealing with misbehaving children in public. *Is it the right thing to do? What if someone sees us?* It's almost as if having to correct a child in public is an admission of failure as a parent. This should not be the case, but it is.

It can be quite embarrassing to enforce even the simplest rule in public, even with a sound and well conceived plan. I once accompanied a friend and his six-year-old son to the supermarket. I was very impressed when before entering the store my friend explained to the child that they were not going to buy any candy. He went even further and explained that if, the child (Andy) insisted on getting candy, he would have to bring him back to the car where they would sit for a few minutes until Andy was ready to return to the store. I thought this was great. My friend had done a good job explaining the situation (rules) as well as the consequences for not following the rules. Then came the trip into the store. Andy headed straight for the candy and grabbed the M&Ms (peanuts in one hand, and plain in the other). Dad closed in from behind and reminded him of the consequences of insisting on candy. Andy broke into a tantrum, but maintained his composure enough to keep a firm grip on the M&Ms. Following through with his plan, my now abashed friend carried Andy kicking and screaming through the store and out to the car, followed by a cashier who wanted to know who would pay for the M&Ms that still couldn't be pried away from Andy.

Obviously, even the best strategies of discipline aren't so easily implemented in supermarkets or any other public setting, especially when you catch a glimpse of your pastor on the next aisle just as you grab your child. Or, when you have to chase your little ones through the produce, before persuading them to stop bowling with oranges. The logistics of implementing a good system of discipline become much more difficult outside of the controlled comfort and privacy of your home.

Children are apt to seek out the limits of any situation. Whenever there is the possibility that the limits may be more flexible than usual, children are quick to check them out and see just how far they can stretch the system. Most systems of discipline bend more in public than in private. However, the testing of rules and limits in public situations is only one explanation for the increase in uncontrollable behavior exhibited by children outside of the confines of home.

Who's in Charge?

The second explanation has to do with who's in charge. Systems of discipline are adversely affected when there are different rules that are in effect in different situations, and when different people are present. Any time there are two different systems of discipline in effect there is the potential for neither to be effective. Parents with children in child care should be quick to recognize this problem. The transition times, when children are dropped off at child care or when they are picked up, can be horrible experiences. Mainly because it is very unclear who is in charge. Many parents won't take full charge and implement their standard system of discipline in the presence of the child care provider, and providers are not always willing to enforce their system while the parent is around.

Here's a typical example. A parent picked up her child from the child care where I was consulting. Earlier in the day the child had lost her privileges on the sliding board outside because she insisted on climbing up the board rather than sliding down. The child care provider had established a safety rule prohibiting climbing up the board. As soon as the girl's mom arrived, the youngster grabbed her hand and led her to the sliding board. With one eye on the child care provider and one eye on her mom, the girl began climbing up the slide pulling her mom along as she went. The mom found this entertaining and accompanied her daughter all the way to the top of the slide. The child care provider never pointed out the rule to the child or the mom. The child was very proud of herself, and not just for climbing the slide.

Many of us have experienced similar phenomena in our professional lives. Having multiple supervisors or bosses is not unlike the child care situation. Having more than one boss can be as good as being without a boss. With the proper motivation, it can be quite easy to play one boss against the other. If there is no clear line of authority and neither boss is really sure about who is in charge, you can spend a lot of time taking advantage of the situation.

A similar situation arises in the presence of relatives. More specifically, grandparents. Rarely, do our methods of discipline and child rearing attain the approval of our parents. Even when we treat our children as our parents treated us, these methods are not always good enough for their grandchildren. Most parents have

stories about grandparents that promote behaviors in children that would have led to corporal punishment when these same grandparents were acting as parents (could they be doing this just to get even).

Even at the risk of stereotyping, I am confident that most grandparents have more flexible standards of behavior, are more easily manipulated by children, and have a more lax system of discipline than parents. This is probably as it should be, but it does create unique problems when children are in the presence of both their grandparents and parents. Grandparents and parents alike are quick to state, *"They only act this way when you are around."* More accurately, an outside observer might notice that, *"They only act that way when both parents and grandparents are around."*

Rules and Consequences

The problem with behavior around grandparents (when parents are present) and the problem with behavior in supermarkets (and other public places) can be traced to the same source. These are times when there is some ambiguity about the rules and the consequences for breaking the rules. Systems of discipline in these situations are very unclear. Who's in charge? Which rules are in effect and which are not? What are the consequences of not following the rules? All of these questions are posed when there is uncertainty about the system of discipline that is in effect.

When parents' hands are even loosely bound together, whether at the supermarket or Grandma's, young children have no remorse in taking full advantage of the situation. Yet, there must be a remedy. Children need exposure to public places, their grandparents, and other adult role models, and they need to learn how to control their own behavior while in these diverse settings.

Occasionally I witness model behavior from young children in public places (sometimes even demonstrated by my own children). What magic is there in these brief moments when parents actually feel like they will escape from the scene without tears shed or broken glass?

While I have not completely mastered the art of taking young children to the supermarket, Grandma's, or other enticing places, I have observed enough failure and success to offer the following advice.

Set the Ground Rules

It is easier to explain ground rules before the game begins than sometime during the first inning. Tell children, what is expected in detail, and explain the consequences of meeting or not meeting these expectations. State any rewards that they can expect for appropriate behavior. Likewise, make sure that they understand the punishment that will accompany inappropriate behavior. Whatever your strategy, getting it out in the open in advance will replace the bribes and threats that are often used as last resorts to terminate unwanted behaviors.

Enforcement Without Exception

Once expectations and consequences have been stated they should be enforced. If the expectations are too high, or the consequences unrealistic, change them for the <u>next</u> outing. They cannot be effectively changed at the check-out counter. It is critical to enforce expectations by following through with consequences. If punishment has been *"promised,"* administer it. If rewards are in order, pay up.

If a healthy discussion in the back seat of the car will terminate an undesired behavior, do it. The embarrassment experienced while my friend carried Andy kicking-and-screaming to the car will be mild compared to the agony of trying to eliminate the same behavior after it has been tolerated a few times.

The opposite is also true. If you have relinquished your system of discipline, (that is, your system is not in effect, either because you are in a situation where you cannot enforce the rules, or someone else has been put in charge) then you cannot change your mind when you see a behavior that you do not like and expect to immediately regain control. This can get tricky. Especially if you see a behavior which you really cannot tolerate. At these times you must decide if this is a battle that you really want to fight.

Can Punishment and Reinforcement Wait?

Parents who find themselves in situations where they feel like they cannot respond immediately to the behavior of their children have the option of dealing with the behavior at a later time, providing they do not forget. Most children are capable of waiting for a reasonable period of time for their reward or punishment and still be affected by the consequences. Psychologists and other "experts" used to think that the consequences of a behavior needed to be experienced immediately in order to be effective. This still

holds true for rats and lower level animals, but fortunately not for human beings. A loss of privilege does not have to occur in the store in order to be effective. Similarly, rewards for good behavior do not have to come in the form of candy at the check-out counter. Parents can wait for a more appropriate time for punishing or rewarding behavior and still have an impact providing the time that elapses is not too long, generally within the same day.

Communicating Expectations

Constant Feedback   In addition to waiting to deliver rewards and punishments, parents can talk to children about their behavior in the store and at Grandma's and let them know how they feel about the way they behaved. Even though parents may let grandma be in charge while at Grandma's house, a good debriefing of what went well and what did not can be useful after the family gets back home. I find these discussions of behavior to be very informative. Sometimes my children are not aware of things that they did at Grandma's that bothered me. Sometimes, I am not aware of things that I did that bothered them. And sometimes, they point out things that they think bothered me, but I overlooked or was not concerned about. Regardless, we come away from these sessions more aware of the expectations that we have for one another.

Looking Ahead   Another important point to remember is that young children do not always have a good sense of time and purpose, particularly in new settings. They may not fully under-stand the sequence of events that is going to occur during a given outing. Sometimes these misconceptions contribute to their behav-ior. They may not understand that there are events that can help them figure out how long a particular experience will last, and how long they might have to endure an unendurable situation.

Children should be told the likely sequence of events to occur in every new public outing. For example, prior to the supermarket trip a child could be told, "*We are going to pick out some fruit and vegetables, get some meat from the butcher, and then head for the check-out counter.*" This type of forewarning allows children to better predict the timing and sequence of activities, and reduces uncertainty about the experience.

Idle hands are the (little) devil's workshop. Even the young-est child can be given something constructive to do while in the supermarket, Grandma's house, or other public places. In the

supermarket they can be responsible for holding the toilet tissue, selecting bananas, pushing the cart, or counting grapes. Some restaurateurs have figured this out and provide crayons with place mats for drawing. It's a great idea. I've found myself asking about the availability of crayolas when making dinner reservations.

Providing meaningful activities for children also gives them a sense of accomplishment and provides parents appropriate behaviors to praise or reward. Parents who are busy praising the accomplishments of their children rarely have the time or need to punish undesired behaviors.

Children will learn to control behavior in diverse settings when they learn that you, and others, hold expectations in these settings that are just as important as your expectations at home. Take control and enforce your expectations, or give over the reins of discipline and let Grandma do it. You'll be amazed at the respect and appreciation bestowed upon you by Grandma and your fellow shoppers.

Activities for Chapter 4

After reading the story ask your child the following questions.

1. What did Abear and Weebear do in the story that they might have done differently?

Your child may need a little time to come up with something. Let your child point out everything that is important. If your child seems confused, try to ask the question a different way. "What kinds of decisions did Abear and Weebear make? Did they do things that bothered Mom or Grandma?" Help your child recognize that:

    a. Abear and Weebear destroyed something precious to Grandma.

    b. Abear and Weebear took advantage of Grandma.

    c. Abear and Weebear may have known that the consequences were different at Grandma's house.

    d. Abear and Weebear disappointed their parents and Grandma.

Reward all ideas with praise. Be open to discuss anything about the story that your child finds interesting. Get information about your child's perspective of the problem. Add your own thoughts about the bears' behavior and what happened.

2. What could Mom, Dad, or Grandma have done differently?

See if your child can identify things in the story that could have been done by the grown-up bears to help avoid the problem. Give your child an opportunity to talk about what Mom, Dad, and Grandma might have done differently. Point out the following:

    a. Mom and Dad could have used their rules at Grandma's house and been clear about who was in charge.

    b. Grandma could have watched the bears more closely.

    c. Grandma could have told the bears to stay away from the paintings.

    d. Mom, Dad, and Grandma could have talked to the bears about the rules at Grandma's, and Mom and Dad could have helped enforce the rules.

3. What should happen to Abear and Weebear? Should Grandma have punished the bears? What should Mom and Dad do? What should happen before they go to Grandma's house again?

Art Activity

Draw a picture of what happens next in the story. Finish the story. Follow one of these options:

    a. You and your child can draw a picture together.

    b. You and your child can draw your own pictures and then compare them.

Whether you draw a picture together or separately be sure to keep an ongoing discussion of the things being drawn. Have your child tell the end of the story using the picture that was drawn.

Parent Homework

Identifying difficult situations is important. Planning ahead can solve many problems. Your homework for this week is to prepare for difficult situations and communicate this plan to your child.

Step 1   Make a list of situations where it is difficult to enforce limits that you have placed on your child. Try to think of at least three to five situations. These might include stores, restaurants,

church, relatives' houses, etc. Rank these situations starting with the most difficult situation.

Step 2   Take your most difficult situation and try to describe the difficulty. Answer these questions. Is your normal system of discipline in place? Is there something about this situation that makes you less consistent? Is it clear who is responsible for evaluating your child's behavior and delivering consequences?

Step 3   Select one of the "problems" identified in Step 2 and devise a plan to fix this problem. If your child needs to know that you are going to be consistent regardless of the public nature of the place, communicate this information and stick to it. Communicate your plan clearly to your child and try it out.

Chapter 5
Gathering Information

One of the best public service spots ever made for television aired in the 1970's. You might remember it. It was simple, a blank screen and a voice that said, "It's 11:00 p.m., do you know where your child is?" At the time I didn't think much about it. It was too obvious, everyone should know their child's whereabouts at 11:00 p.m. But, keeping up with your children involves much more than knowing their location at night or any other time. Supervising and keeping up with your child depends on the ability to gather information.

Gathering good information about your child's behavior is very important in developing a system of discipline and guidance. In the discussion of discipline presented in Chapter 2, the importance of a comprehensive and consistent system of discipline was explained. There are clear goals (or rules) to be achieved, and consistent consequences for achieving or not achieving these goals. The ability to gather information about a child's behavior contributes directly to the comprehensiveness and consistency of a system of discipline in the following ways.

Information to Set Goals

A good system of discipline includes goals for a wide range of situations. Parents who are implementing such a system must obtain enough information to help them establish these goals. Goals to be obtained in a comprehensive discipline system can be thought of as targets for change. If a parent notices something that needs to be changed, they can identify this as a target behavior for change and put together an appropriate strategy for changing the behavior. But, the first step is recognizing the specific behavior that needs changing.

Obtaining the information necessary to develop strategies for change is not always easy. Suppose you become concerned

about your child's diet. You suspect a problem in eating balanced meals, even though all four food groups are available at every meal. You decide to make some improvements. What should be your goal? Should you encourage your child to eat more of everything? Should you focus on vegetables? Or, should you set a goal for finishing everything on the plate?

Before deciding on a specific goal you need more information. For starters, you would need to know how much your child is currently eating, as well as what they are eating. The amount and type of food being eaten may be perfectly adequate, or there may be room for improvement. An acheivable goal can be set when you have gathered the basic information about the problem. You may find your child is eating very few, if any, vegetables. If so, it may not be realistic to immediately set a goal that requires vegetables to be eaten at every meal. A more realistic starting point would be to eat at least one serving of vegetables per day. However, you need the basic information on exactly what is being eaten before you can make these specific plans for change. You are then in a position to use this information to further develop and modify goals.

Information to Determine Consequences

Once you have established solid goals, good information is needed to determine whether or not these goals are being accomplished. Keeping up with changes that have or have not occurred gives you feedback about the success of your plan. Goals (or target behaviors) are affected by what children experience when they succeed or fail in accomplishing the goal. Parents can influence what children experience in relation to a goal. They can reward accomplishments, provide mild punishment for not achieving the goal, or simply ignore behaviors. But, parents can only influence those behaviors of which they are aware. It is impossible to reward or punish a behavior (or the lack of a behavior) unless you know that it happened or did not happen.

We sometimes set up goals about which information is difficult to gather. These behaviors are either hard to observe or difficult to obtain accurate information about by asking questions. Consistency is impossible when behaviors that are targets to be changed go unrecognized. Suppose you are concerned about your children's behavior while they are with a new, and inexperienced baby sitter. You observe that upon returning home, the sitter always looks frazzled and the house is a wreck. You decide that

your expectations are for your children to do everything that they are told to do by the sitter. This is probably not a very good goal to start with, but one that I have sometimes stated myself. The next time you return home, the house looks just as bad, and the sitter looks worse. When you ask the sitter whether or not the children complied with her every command, the sitter says they did. When you ask the children you get the same reply.

The problem is either the sitter does not care how bad things get for her or the house and she hasn't asked the children to do anything, or you have established a goal that is nearly impossible to monitor. The sitter is probably embarrassed to admit that she cannot make the children do anything. As long as the sitter will not confess, the children are not about to admit to misbehaving. Perhaps a goal of not having the house look like a tornado struck would be more appropriate and easier to monitor. This goal could be monitored after the fact. If you come home and the house and sitter are a wreck, you can take action and stand a chance of changing the behavior.

Information on Rewards and Punishment

Finally, parents who are providing consequences for achieving or not achieving goals need to gather information about the effects of the consequences they have chosen. We assume, as parents, that we know what motivates our children, and often our assumptions are correct. I recently offered the following deal to my children. My spouse and I wanted to play tennis at a place that has a swimming pool and a small playground for children. The deal was that if the children would play quietly while we played tennis (specifically without fighting or asking when we were going to be done), then we would take them swimming. Since they love swimming, I assumed that it would be a good reward for not disturbing our tennis game. I was right. They were great and we had a wonderful time swimming afterward.

But, what if they had not achieved the goal of not bothering us every two minutes? There would be two explanations for their noncompliance. First, it could be that I have a history of inconsistency in following through with consequences. Given that I am writing this book, let's assume that I have been consistent and that this first explanation isn't plausible. The second explanation is that the reward that I offered (swimming) was not enticing enough to get the kids to leave us alone. Sometimes the consequences that

follow a behavior are not sufficient to change the behavior, even if it seems like they should.

Consider sending a child to their room as a consequence of misbehaving. If their room is filled with exciting things to do, this punishment is not likely to work. They love it there. It's like throwing Brer Rabbit into the briar patch. Two simple rules about changing behavior can help.

Rule 1: Anything which follows a behavior and increases the chance of that behavior occurring in the future is a reward for that behavior.

Rule 2: Anything which follows a behavior and decreases the chance of that behavior occurring in the future is a punishment for that behavior.

When following these simple rules, there are no such things as rewards and punishments that don't work. Parents have often told me, *"I rewarded and rewarded, and I punished and I punished, and that kid hasn't changed a bit."* This is not possible using the above mentioned rules. These parents are providing consequences for behavior that they think will change the behavior of their children. But if their children's behavior is not changing, and they are being consistent, then they have not found the right rewards and punishments.

So, how do you know if the rewards and punishments that you have established are working? Simple, you continue to gather information on the behavior that you are trying to change. If you observe that the behavior is decreasing when you provide certain consequences, then these consequences are punishing the behavior. If you observe that the behavior that you want to change is increasing, then the consequences that you are providing are rewarding this behavior. It's simple, but the key, however, is gathering the right type of information.

Two Ways to Gather Information

What can be done to get the information? There are two ways of getting information about behaviors and the consequences that follow them. 1) You can observe the behaviors and their consequences directly, (using all of your senses), or 2) you can ask someone about these behaviors and their consequences. Both methods provide valuable information.

47

Observing Observing behavior is the best place to start. Parents can simply look, listen, smell, taste, or feel their way into better information. Granted the smell, taste and feel will be used less often than the looking and listening. Systematically observing behavior is not always as simple as it seems. There are, however, three techniques for observing behavior that can make the job easier.

1. <u>Know what you are looking for</u>. Be specific in what you are trying to observe. Whether you are obtaining information to help establish a goal, modify a behavior to achieve the goal, or evaluate the effectiveness of a reward or punishment, there needs to be something very specific that you are observing. It helps to write down the behavior that you want changed using as much detail as possible.

2. <u>Find out exactly how many times the behavior is occurring</u>. There are some things that annoy parents that happen all the time, there are other things that happen infrequently, but are very annoying. To change behavior and evaluate the effectiveness of your plan for changing the behavior, you need to have a good idea of the rate of the behavior (how many times it is actually happening). Once you have charted how many times something happens then you can make better decisions. Again, it is helpful to keep track, on paper, of the number of times the behavior happens. Our memories are not always helpful. This is especially true for behaviors that don't happen often, but are very annoying when they do occur. We usually think that this type of behavior is happening much more frequently than it actually occurs.

3. <u>Don't try to observe too many things at any one time</u>. Observe one or two specific behaviors at a time. Sometimes it is tempting to decide that you are going to *"fix everything that I don't like about this kid's behavior."* This can lead to getting a lot of information, with none of it very good or useful. Select one or two good targets for observation and track these behaviors for several days. Once you are satisfied with the results and the type of information that you are receiving, you might reduce the formality of observing these behaviors and focus on other targets for change.

Asking Another method of obtaining information about behavior is to ask about it, or be told about it. This requires open lines of communication. Open communication between parents and children can facilitate information gathering tremendously. There would be no need for direct observation of children's behav-

ior if they could and would accurately report on everything that is happening in their life (wishful thinking, right?).

Systematically observing children's behavior and keeping the lines of communication open are not always compatible. A dramatic increase in one of these methods may lead to decreases in the other. A child whose behavior is constantly observed (to the point that every move is being written down), may react by closing off lines of communication in order to obtain a tiny bit of privacy. On the other hand, a parent with a child who seems to be spontaneously reporting on every possible behavior, may become lax in their direct observations of those behaviors.

Directly observing behaviors and communicating effectively should be used in combination to develop a good style of obtaining information. Over-reliance on either method of obtaining information can lead to problems. As children get older both strategies will be helpful in dealing with behaviors that get progressively more difficult to supervise. Unfortunately, older children tell you less, and do less in front of you that you can observe. You will need skill in both direct observation and communication to obtain the information that you need to make parenting decisions.

Pitfalls

There are two pitfalls of information gathering that need to be mentioned before closing this section. First, many parents have a tendency to closely monitor undesired behavior and not pay much attention to the "good" behaviors that are being exhibited. These good behaviors need to be rewarded as consistently as the "bad" behaviors are punished. There is a general tendency to let good behaviors turn into expectations that go unrewarded. After these behaviors happen a few times we just expect that they always will. Somehow, it is easier to spot those behaviors that need to be terminated before spotting those behaviors that need promoting. Trying to establish a balance of information on the good and the bad avoids establishing a system that is always correcting and never encouraging behaviors. Once such a negative system is developed it is unpleasant for both parents and child, and becomes difficult to change.

The second danger of close supervision is finding out something that you really did not want to know. Sometimes when you start taking a really close look at a behavior, or you start asking probing questions, you find out disturbing things. You may find

that there are things you have always thought were rewarding to your child that are not very rewarding at all. Or, you may find out that those behaviors that you find so aggravating don't happen very much, and when they do there is usually a good reason. Or, you may find that there are behaviors that are very difficult to change regardless of the consequences. All of these findings can be put to good use. Nonetheless, they can be disturbing to parents.

The benefits of gathering good information easily outweigh these minor pitfalls. When you become skilled in gathering information on your child you are well on your way to establishing a system of working with your child to obtain a harmonious relationship.

Activities for Chapter 5

After reading the story ask your child the following questions.

1. What was Abear's problem?

Give your child plenty of time to come up with an answer. Ask if there are any other things that Abear could have done differently. If your child seems confused, try to ask the question a different way. "What did Abear do that he might want to change?" Help your child recognize that:

a. Abear's Mom did not recognize his clean room.
b. Abear did not tell his Mom that he had cleaned his room.
c. Abear let Bearly talk him into doing something that he did not really want to do.
d. Abear messed up his room before Mom had a chance to tell him how nice it looked.

Praise any attempts to describe Abear's actions. Generate a discussion of how Abear felt about his Mom not seeing his room immediately. Try to get information from your child's perspective. Add your own thoughts about Abear's behavior.

2. What could Mom and Dad have done differently?

Paying attention to both the good and the bad is important. Give your child an opportunity to talk about what Mom might have done differently. Point out the following:

a. Mom could have looked in on Abear to see his room.

b. Dad could have praised Abear for his room before telling Mom.

c. Mom could have immediately told Abear how proud she was about his room, rather than waiting to fix a special dinner.

3. What should Mom and Dad do about Abear's room? Should they make him clean it again? Should they let him eat his special dinner? Should Mom apologize for not seeing the room? Should they all work together and clean his room, and enjoy the nice meal?

4. What could the bears do differently in the future?

Help your child decide things that the family might do to avoid these kinds of situations. Start by talking about ways that they could keep up with "room cleaning". Abear could write down every day that his room is clean, putting the information on a chart for his mother. Abear's mom could check every day to see if Abear's room is clean. Abear could tell Mom and Dad when he finishes picking up his room.

Art Activity

Draw a picture of what happens after Abear sees the dinner and his parents see his messy room. Follow one of these options:

a. You and your child can draw a picture together.

b. You and your child can draw your own pictures and then compare them.

Whether you draw a picture together or separately be sure to keep an ongoing discussion of the things being drawn. Have your child tell the end of the story using the picture that was drawn.

Parent Homework

Your homework for this chapter will be gathering information by observing and asking questions. The purpose is to use good observation and communication skills to gather as much information as possible.

Step 1   Choose a behavior that you would like to have more information about, and that you can easily observe. This should be something that happens enough to keep a record of over the period of a week. *Examples: bed making, picking up clothes, arguing with siblings, whining.* Try to write down a clear definition of this behavior (be very specific).

Step 2   Think of a way to keep track of the behavior that you have chosen. This could be a chart or something like the form presented in Chapter 2. Try out different things. The goal is to develop a method of gathering accurate information on the behavior.

Step 3   Next, choose a behavior that is difficult for you to observe. Select a behavior that you will need to ask about, something that happens at school or that happens in their friends' homes. *Examples: manners away from home, schoolwork and activities, personal hygiene habits.* Practice the good communication skills presented earlier to get the best information possible about the selected behavior. Use probing questions and good listening skills. You may want to ask others about the behavior in addition to your child. Asking teachers and friends about the same behavior is a good way to determine how much you are actually being told by your child.

Step 4   Develop a method for recording the information that you obtain. You will need this record to see any changes in the behavior. Be creative. Think of ways of recording this information (chart, shorthand notes, etc.) that are efficient and informative.

Chapter 6
Sharing and Caring

Sometimes young children can seem like the most selfish and insensitive creatures on earth. That's because in a way they are. The famous Swiss psychologist, Jean Piaget, labeled this state in children *"egocentric"*. Piaget explained this egocentric state as the inability to take the perspective of another person, and claimed that this inability is responsible for what appears to be selfishness and insensitivity to the plight of others. It is not that young children do not want to take another person's point of view, it's simply that they can't.

Three Mountains and Egocentrism

Piaget illustrated this inability in what he called *"the three mountain task"*. Picture three miniature mountains lined up on a table. One mountain is large, the next is a bit smaller, and the third is still smaller. If a person sits at the table in front of the large mountain, their view of the other two mountains is obstructed by the size of the large mountain in front of them. If the same person sits on the opposite side of the table (the side closest to the small mountain), they are able to see all three mountains with each getting progressively larger.

The task begins by seating a three or four-year-old child in front of the large mountain and an adult in front of the small mountain. The adult asks the child,*"How many mountains do you see?"* The child says, *"One."* *"How many mountains do I see?"* the adult asks. *"One,"* replies the child.

They then switch seats and the adults asks, *"Now, how many mountains do you see?"* The child says, *"Three."* *"Well, how many mountains do I see now?"* continues the adult. *"Three,"* states the child emphatically. The bewildered adult then says, *"But when you were on this side you could see only one mountain."* *"Right,"* replies the child not noticing any inconsitency in logic.

53

The apparent selfishness and lack of concern for others that children sometimes display can be accounted for in large part by this egocentric view of the world. It is not that young children lack the motivation to take the other person's point of view, it's simply that they don't think that way. They have one basic way of looking at the world, through their own eyes. This has major implications for the types of things that can be expected of children in their relationships with parents, other children, and their siblings.

Establishing successful relationships with other people is partially dependent upon the ability to take the other person's point of view and respond accordingly. Using positive and supportive behaviors in relationships (sometimes referred to as prosocial or helping behaviors) often requires taking the other person's point of view. Sharing and cooperating with other children is most affected by this perspective taking ability (or inability).

Sharing

It is great to see kids share and it is a value that most parents try to instill in their children. But, realistically, young children are not very good at sharing, especially spontaneous sharing, or sharing and not immediately expecting something in return (commonly referred to as altruism). It is common to see children as old as eight or nine share something with their friend, but leave their hand extended while asking when they can have it back. While most kids this age are becoming less and less egocentric, the remnants of this view of the world makes it very difficult for children to share without expecting an immediate pay back. Children are often looking for a reward for sharing, even if they do not request it from their peers. Children will often share with a peer, then report that they shared to their parents and expect exuberant praise -- hardly the most noble intentions.

Cooperating

Cooperation requires taking turns and working together to complete a task. This might mean not always getting to do what you like, and being sensitive to the contributions of other people. This requires taking the perspective of the person with whom you are cooperating. Consequently the amount of true cooperation between children is limited. In Chapter 3 the term *"fairweather cooperation"* was introduced. This term characterized children's friendships on the basis of the immediate benefits of interacting with one another. There is cooperation in these relationships, but

only when the benefits of this cooperation are obvious to both participants. Cooperation breaks down when it is not obvious to one of the kids interacting that there is something to be gained.

Aggressive Behavior

Negative behaviors in early childhood are also influenced by egocentrism. Children who hit other children without regard for the way that these children feel, are egocentric. Children who snatch toys from other children without noticing that it pushes their playmate into a tantrum, are egocentric. They lack empathy. Sometimes parents and teachers are unrealistic in thinking that simply pointing out the reaction of other children will somehow cure this egocentric condition.

Following an incident where one child has attacked another to get a giant tinker toy, a teacher approaches the offender and asks, *"Why did you hit Tim? Can't you see that you made him cry?"* To which the offender responds, *"Yea, but I got the tinker toy."* The toy snatcher was successful in getting the toy and is relatively happy. In his egocentric view of the world why should it matter to him that the other child is in tears.

Luckily most children eventually develop less egocentric ways of looking at the world (although we can all name adults who do not seem to have progressed very far in this arena). How do children begin to develop this appreciation for the other person's perspective? Does it just happen? Or, are there things that parents can do to help it happen? It's actually a little of both.

Helping Children Take a Different Point of View

As children get older they begin to develop the cognitive (mental) ability to take the point of view of other children. This is a somewhat naturally occurring development. But, some children outgrow egocentrism more rapidly and completely than others. There are some very specific activities that can stimulate movement away from egocentric thought and into better relationships with adults and other children.

Same-Aged Peers The first step is to provide opportunities for children to interact with a variety of same-aged peers. The importance of such interactions was stated in Chapter 3, and is even more significant when considering the importance of practice in taking the point of view of a peer.

A child gets a certain amount of practice interacting with parents, but there is a different quality about these relationships.

For one thing, parents tend to adjust their point of view to fit the point of view of their children, more than children are apt to modify their perspective to be consistent with their parent's. It is simply easier for parents to adjust their perspective.

A child playing with a peer cannot depend on the peer to adapt to his/her perspective. The peer is no better at this thing called perspective taking than the child. Therefore, there is considerably more equality in the give and take in same-aged relationships than there is in parent-child relations.

Another quality of parent-child relations that makes them unique from peer relations is that they are somewhat permanent. A child who refuses to take their parents' point of view is not risking losing their parent. However, with peer relations the issues are different. With peers there is always the possibility of terminating the relationship by refusing to take the other person's perspective.

Suppose two children are playing on a preschool playground. One young girl has been swinging for several minutes while her playmate has waited quietly for a turn. The waiting girl finally asks for a turn and the swinging girl refuses to give up the swing. Chances are the waiting girl will simply leave. It is easy to see that not sharing puts the entire relationship in jeopardy. Children who have a lot of experience interacting with same-aged playmates begin to understand these concepts more quickly than children who are not exposed to as many children.

Unstructured Time   It is important that a large portion of the time that children have with peers is relatively unstructured. Unstructured activities (like playing outside on the playground, or just hanging out with free time) allow children to negotiate perspectives. These situations are very different than games or activities that have clear rules and perspectives that are not negotiable. Watching children decide what to do with their time together can be fascinating. They each have an idea of what they want to do, and they can spend long periods of time advocating their stand.

Given that young children's first inclination is to see the world their way, they will try to push their perspective from the onset of most interactions. However, in unstructured activities other children have the opportunity to "*sell*" their perspective as well. The result is a lot of negotiating (sometimes in the form of arguing) points of view. This is very healthy for children. They will learn to advocate for their own position while sometimes accepting the position of others.

Some parents and educators are not comfortable letting kids just *"hang out"*. They think that unstructured time is unproductive time, or that if kids are given too much time without anything specific to do they will get into some kind of trouble. This simply is not true. But, if you just can't stand it, and you think that interaction opportunities need to be more structured, there are two simple points to remember.

Limiting Resources The first point is that limited resources challenge children to resolve issues that can lead to sharing and cooperation. This simply means that children will be forced to share and cooperate more when there are not enough resources to go around. These resources could be toys, time, or turns at a particular activity. Not much sharing or cooperating occurs when there is enough of everything for everybody. Sharing and cooperating are only necessary when there are limited resources. If there were twenty identical sets of everything in a first grade classroom with twenty students, the students would share very few materials. Likewise, when siblings have matched pairs of everything, they rarely see the need to share with one another.

On the other hand, if there are few resources available, and a group of children really want access to these resources, then interesting group dynamics emerge. Children can do two things when they are faced with limited resources. They can fight over them and have every person fend for themselves, or they can develop a fair system of distributing these resources. Even without adult intervention, over time most children will devise a relatively fair way to share resources.

There is, however, a danger of promoting a very competitive environment when limiting the resources available to children. Children are naturally competitive with one another. Establishing environments with limited resources might lead to intense competition for these resources.

Rewarding Joint Behavior Competitive environments can be avoided by one simple technique -- reward group accomplishments instead of individual ones. The result is teamwork rather than competition. Group rewards lead to cooperation and helping, individual rewards lead to competition and conflict.

Limiting resources and rewarding group accomplishments can work together to create very important opportunities for children to learn to share and cooperate. For the past year or so I have regularly conducted *"Dad's Coloring Contest"*. There are several

versions of the contest, two of which are excellent illustrations of how slight differences in structure influence social interaction. The basic idea of all of the contests is that the children color pictures, I judge the pictures, and distribute prizes under various categories (most colorful, best staying in the lines, best getting out of the lines, etc.).

In one version of the game I give each child their own box of crayons (the big 64 color version), their own picture to color, and I judge each of their pictures separately before distributing the prizes. In the other version of the game, I give them three crayons (total) one picture to color, and judge this picture to determine if it is worthy of a prize. The number of prizes that the kids receive always ends up about the same regardless of the type contest.

But, there are very different things that happen during the contest. When there are ample crayons (resources) and each child is trying to win a certain prize (individual reward) there is a lot of competition, very little positive interaction during the contest, and usually a lot of dissatisfaction with the distribution of prizes. When the crayons and pictures are limited, and the prizes are awarded based on the qualities of only one picture, the children share the three crayons, they compliment each others' work, they give each other suggestions for improving their work, and generally they get along better. At the end of these limited resources and group rewarded contests the kids are always more pleased with the prize, and usually end up sharing their prizes.

It amazes me. Each version of the contest takes the same amount of time and energy, and the end result in terms of prizes is the same. But, the structure of the situation has a dramatic impact on the social interaction that emerges during the contest.

Practice Makes Perfect Children need as much practice in demonstrating positive social behaviors as is possible. Providing ample opportunities to practice sharing, by giving your children exposure to other children in structured and unstructured situations should be a high priority for parents.

Through experience children will begin to see the value of their social contributions to others. They will begin to recognize that the returns on sharing with and helping other children, will come in the form of friendship and more opportunities to interact with their favorite peers.

Children become more socially competent by practicing social skills with peers. However, it takes good initial relationships

with peers in order to have someone with whom to practice. In social development the competent children tend to get more competent by virtue of the increasing contact that they have with other competent children. The incompetent fall further behind because their limited skills do not attract many children with whom to practice and improve these skills.

Children's social development tends to flow either upward or downward because of the role that social skills play in attracting practice partners. The earlier parents begin stimulating the social experiences of their children, the better chance they have to get children moving upward in a cycle toward social competence in adulthood.

Activities for Chapter 6

Discuss the Storybook chapter using the following questions as guidelines.

1. What did Abear and Weebear do in the story that they might have done differently?

Ask your child to think of as many things as possible that Abear and Weebear did that they could have done differently. If your child seems confused, repeat the question a different way. "What did Abear and Weebear do to make each other angry?" Help your child recognize that:

    a. Abear and Weebear did not cooperate with the net.

    b. They took turns, but they could have worked together and gotten more fish.

    c. They were so busy fighting that the fish got away.

    d. They tore the net because of their argument.

Praise any attempts to describe Abear and Weebear's behavior. Start a discussion of Abear and Weebear's problems. Try to get information from your child about their perspective of the problem. Add your own thoughts.

2. What could the two bears do next time?

How might they avoid these kinds of situations? What could they do the next time they have a chance to work together, or to share? Give your child time to come up with ideas and then point out the following:

a. Abear and Weebear could have worked together to catch lots of fish.
b. Abear and Weebear could have taken turns, with one catching fish and the other holding the fish they had already caught.
c. They could have been more careful with the fish and the net.
d. They could have been kinder and more supportive to one another, not laughing and teasing each other.

3. **What should Abear and Weebear do with their last fish? Should they give it to the old bear and try to catch another, even though they no longer have the net? Should they try to help the old bear catch some fish? Should they give him their fish <u>and</u> try to help him catch some more?**

Art Activity

Draw a picture of what Abear and Weebear decide to do about the fish. Follow one of these options:
a. You and your child can draw a picture together.
b. You and your child can draw your own pictures and then compare them.

Whether you draw a picture together or separately be sure to keep an ongoing discussion of the things being drawn. Have your child tell the end of the story using the picture that was drawn.

Parent Homework

Your homework for this chapter is to experiment with situations that promote sharing and cooperation. The purpose is for your children to get some practice sharing and cooperating, and for you to see the impact that small changes in setting up activities have on sharing and cooperating.

Step 1 Set up a *"free play situation"* where you can observe (five or ten minutes is all you need to watch) your child and friend(s). Write down every instance of sharing or cooperating.

Step 2   Suggest to your children and their friends that they have a contest with rewards. You can use the coloring contest that I described or any other activity that is suited for both individual and group work. Have the children do the activity giving them plenty of resources to work with on their own. Reward one *"winner"* with a desirable prize. Tell the children beforehand that their will be only one winner.   Again, write down every instance of sharing or cooperating.

Step 3   Have one more contest. This time tell the children that you want one *"product"* from the group, and if it meets your standards (whatever they may be) each of them will receive a reward. Limit the resources that are available to the children to finish the product. Make it necessary to share resources. One more time, write down every instance of sharing or cooperating.

Step 4   Compare the amount of sharing and cooperating that you observed in each of Steps 1-3. Make a decision on the types of peer activities you would like to encourage for sharing and cooperation.

Chapter 7
Playing by the Rules

Eventually, we all have to learn to play by the rules. Even though crime rates are high, most of us are not in jail -- evidence that we are at least following the more formalized rules of society. It is amazing that more people do not get into trouble given the number and complexity of rules that exist.

There are a host of different rules that govern our behavior -- both formal and informal rules. Any constraint on behavior can be considered a rule. Situations where some behaviors are allowed and even promoted, and other behaviors are prohibited and punished, involve rules.

Sometimes rules are expressly written and formally enforced, such is the case with laws and the judicial system which enforces them. But other rules are less formalized, not always expressly stated, and the enforcement of these rules is not always clearly visible. Nonetheless, these informal rules play a major role in maintaining order and avoiding chaos in our world.

One set of informal rules are those that control our social behavior. These rules govern what is appropriate in getting along with other human beings. People often develop very complex, informal social rules. The consequences of consistently breaking these rules is social condemnation or rejection. For example, you are at a restaurant with someone that you just met. The server brings your drinking water and your new acquaintance begins pouring it over his hands and scrubbing up for the meal. When the food arrives your guest shuns the utensils and digs into his spaghetti and sauce with his now clean fingers. How likely is it that you will join this person for dinner in the near future?

Using your drinking water to cleanse hands, and eating spaghetti and meat sauce with your fingers are relatively mild violations of social rules. It is not quite as bad as swimming naked in a public fountain, but the consequences of breaking even the

mildest social rules can have a dramatic impact on an individual. Given the number of informal rules that exist, and the severe consequences of consistently breaking these rules, understanding the process of learning and abiding by social rules becomes paramount in development.

Socializing Children

Socialization is the process of learning social rules. It begins at birth and lasts a lifetime. The process of socializing children is complex. Everything that a child experiences influences their socialization. Behaviors are governed by the consequences that follow them. Behaviors that are encouraged or rewarded will persist, those that are discouraged, ignored, or punished will cease. Every behavior exhibited by a child receives some sort of reaction from the environment. The first smiles of an infant are met with smiles and shrieks of joy from parents -- more infant smiles follow.

Children learn about their world from the responses that they get from their environment. They learn what is okay and what is not okay. They are, however, active participants in this learning process. They actively participate in their socialization in two important ways.

Creating Social Opportunities   From the earliest days of life the type of behavior exhibited by children influences their environment. Babies who cry a lot usually get held a lot. And once held a lot, they cry to be held more. Socialization is an interactive process. That is, children respond to their environment, their environment responds in turn, and the entire process starts over. This process is largely responsible for shaping the social characteristics of children.

One of the clearest examples of this process can be seen in the interactions of preschool children and their peers. A child who shares and cooperates with peers is rewarded by more opportunities to share and cooperate. The child's behavior (sharing or cooperating in this case) is promoted by an environment (peers in this case) that provides the opportunity for the behavior to occur. Once the behavior occurs (being positive to other kids), the environment (other kids) is more likely to provide the same opportunities in the future. On the other hand children who act negatively to peers (fighting or teasing) quickly find themselves in an environment where they cannot practice more positive behaviors. Children do not want to interact with children who are negative and

abrasive. Consequently, these negative children begin to experience fewer opportunities to interact with other children.

Understanding the Value of Rules   Children also actively participate in their socialization through their contribution to the formation of social rules.   At a very early age children become fascinated with rules, their importance, their meaning, and the extent to which they apply within their world. I once observed a 14-month-old being taught *"not to touch"* certain items in his house. He was becoming familiar with the nasal sound *"ahnnn"* that his parents made instead of saying *"NO!"* Later, in a new environment (my home) he immediately used his understanding (or lack of understanding) of the rules to check out what was appropriate to touch. He would approach every reachable object, hold his hand within an inch of it, look at his mother and say *"ahnnn?"* If Mom echoed the *"ahnnn"* he would leave the object untouched and move to the next closest thing. If mom said nothing he would touch it quickly before moving on to the next item.

This fascination with rules is an important component of socialization. Children start with a very limited understanding of rules and develop quickly into little rule makers -- and breakers -- with very complicated strategies for manipulating social rules.

Psychologist Lawrence Kohlberg described a series of stages that children pass through in developing an understanding of rules and their relevance. According to Dr. Kohlberg, children begin their life without any concept of right and wrong, and have no appreciation for social rules. During this *first stage* of life they are essentially without rules or order.

In the *second stage* of development they begin to learn that there are rules, but only to the extent that there are different consequences associated with breaking these rules. In this early stage of thinking children will suggest that a rule is a rule because breaking it leads to punishment. It will remain a rule as long as punishment is administered when it is broken. To children in this developmental stage, rules that do not have negative consequences must not be rules.

Later, in the *third stage*, children begin to attribute more permanency to rules. In fact, they become quite insistent that a rule is a rule and there are no exceptions. Once stated as a rule, children adhere to it as if it were written in stone. During this stage there is no room for flexibility, even in very ambiguous situations where rule violations are justifiable by adult standards. One such situa-

tion involves intentionality. Children in this stage of understanding would expect a purposeful rule offender to be treated as severely as an offender who unintentionally violated a rule. To this group of children, a rule is a rule is a rule.

Finally, during the *fourth stage*, children come to a more adult-like understanding of rules. They are learning that rules exist to maintain some sort of social order. In this final stage children are capable of understanding that rules are made by people to make their lives more manageable, and can be changed by people.

When children begin to realize that rules are guidelines for behavior that can be constantly modified, they take great pleasure in experimenting with the rules. Not only do they continue to test the limits of many rules, now they are fascinated with creating rules and the consequences that will be associated with breaking these rules. One only needs to observe children organizing a group game to understand their fascination with rule making and rule changing.

Elementary school children are particularly skilled at organizing and reorganizing games and their rules. Sometimes it appears that the game is secondary to the rules and the individual strategies that are developed to modify these rules. It is not uncommon to see children engage in a game where everyone has a turn to play, and everyone has a turn to modify the rules. It reminds me of poker. Poker as a card game has scores of different formats, each with its own set of rules. It is fun to play poker, but it's more fun to play and be the dealer. You see, the dealer gets to choose the format of the game and its corresponding rules. Everyone wants a turn to deal.

A fascination with rules and their purpose is very appropriate developmentally, and indicates a high level of social understanding. Parents can benefit tremendously from understanding the developmental process of rules and their justification. Many behaviors of children can be explained by an understanding of this process, and many strategies for improving parent-child relations depend upon a thorough understanding of these and related issues.

Parents and Rules

Parents who understand the above mentioned stages that children go through in developing an understanding of rules have an advantage. Once you have a better understanding of the way children perceive rules, you can have more realistic expectations

65

about their compliance with the rules. For example, when children are just learning that rules exist, it is not realistic for them to comply just because a rule has been established. However, when children are a little older, they are quick to judge the existence of a rule by the consequences of breaking it. From this child you can expect that inconsistency in enforcing a rule will lead to claims that they did not know it was really a rule.

Most importantly, parents who understand these stages are less shocked by children who suddenly become non-compliant and begin to question authority. These are the four and five-year-old children who want to negotiate a new bedtime, or want to know why every family rule -- stated or unstated -- is in existence. Parents who understand these developmental differences in children can better appreciate the questioning of long standing rules and understand that this fascination with rules is an important advancement in their children. In fact, there are several things that parents can do to promote their children's understanding of rules and their relevance.

Be Consistent Consistency is critical to effective discipline, and it is critical to developing a good understanding of rules and their importance. Inconsistency is very confusing. How can a child learn about rules and their importance, when initially it is very unclear what rules are in effect. Inconsistency is particularly harmful to young children who are in the stage of believing that only rules which are consistently enforced are *"real"* rules. These children think if they break a rule and the consequences of doing so are not negative, then it must not have really been a rule.

Explain Deviations from the Rules It is important to communicate when rules are changed, or temporarily suspended. As was discussed in Chapter 2, there is a tremendous difference between modifying rules and being inconsistent. If there are exceptions for rules, or periods of time when social rules are not in effect (like eating with your fingers on a picnic) make sure that children are aware of these exceptions. Making them aware of these exceptions will avoid the confusion associated with inconsistency, and it will begin to teach them that rules can be modified for the good of the group.

Provide Well Supervised but Unstructured Opportunities for Children and Their Peers   Well supervised but unstructured opportunities encourage children to make up their own rules. Children in unstructured environments will make up their own structure. This includes deciding what to play and constructing any pertinent rules of behavior. Such spontaneous situations are healthy in promoting an understanding of the usefulness of rules.

Encourage Taking the Perspective of the Group   Parents can encourage children to be sensitive to the needs of other children and adults, and to appreciate that rules are meant for the good of the entire group. This means that occasionally they will experience rules that appear to be more advantageous to another child. Cooperative games, those that require two or more children to cooperate in achieving a goal, are very beneficial in the development of perspective taking. Working closely on a common goal can give children insights into the needs of other children much more quickly than can competitive situations.

Allow Input into Family Rules   Children can benefit tremendously from being allowed to have input into a variety of family rules. When children participate in developing family rules (and the consequences of breaking the rules) they begin to understand the reason for rules and their importance in maintaining order within the family. Receiving input into family rules can be achieved through family meetings. In these meetings family members can negotiate rules and rule changes, while learning to communicate with one another more effectively.

Talk About Rules and Their Importance   Keep reminding children that rules are for the good of the entire group. That means that sometimes they won't like the rules. Sometimes it helps to point out situations in which others had to live with rules that best suited your child's behavior.

We sometimes dine at a pizza parlor with a variety of playground equipment for children. There is a sign next to one activity that allows access only to younger children. My older daughter is incensed that she is too tall for the activity and her little sister is not. I have to constantly remind her of the activities (too numerous to mention) which she can do that her sister cannot.

Conclusion

It is amazing how many rules we have for our children. It is not surprising since many of these are for their safety. Remember, your child is just developing an understanding of rules and the consequences for breaking them. You can help them develop a healthy respect and adherence to rules by communicating, and being fair and consistent.

Activities for Chapter 7

After reading the story ask your child the following questions.

1. What happened to Abear in the story?

Ask if there is anything that Abear or his friends could have done differently. Give ample time for your child to come up with answers. If your child seems confused, try to ask the question a different way. Help your child recognize that:

  a. Abear and Bearette could not agree on the card game.
  b. Abear was not sure of the rules and would not listen to Bearette.
  c. The bears tried several different ways to play the rope game.
  d. The bears needed to takes turns with different rules in their games so that everyone would have a chance to do what they wanted.
  e. When Abear decided he wanted to untie the ropes he needed to think about how this changed the rules and made his friends feel.

Praise any attempts to describe the situation. Promote a discussion of the rules of games, trying to get information from your child about their perspective. Add your own thoughts about Abear, Bearly and Bearette's behavior.

2. What should they do about the rope game? Who should decide? Does everyone get to decide? How should they make their decision? What else could the bears do?

3. What can they do next time?

How might the bears avoid these kinds of situations? What could they do the next time they have to decide what game to play

and what the rules of the game will be? Give your child time to come up with ideas and then point out the following:

    a. They could each take turns deciding what to play, understanding that the rules could change with every turn.

    b. They could vote on the game and the rules.

    c. They could look for something completely different to do that they all enjoy.

Art Activity

Draw a picture of what Abear, Bearette, and Bearly decide to do about the jump rope game. Follow one of these options:

    a. You and your child can draw a picture together.

    b. You and your child can draw your own pictures and then compare them.

Whether you draw a picture together or separately be sure to keep an ongoing discussion of the things being drawn. Have your child tell the end of the story using the picture that was drawn.

Parent Homework

This week your homework has two parts. Part One asks you to play a simple game with changing rules, and Part Two asks you to set up a family meeting designed to get input on your own family rules. You may be in the habit of creating games to play with your children, and you may already hold family meetings. If so, use the steps presented to think about your games and meetings and make any needed improvements.

Part 1- The Thinking Game

The Thinking Game has been around a long time. It is a simple game where one person thinks of something (usually writing it down), and then gives other people clues about what they are thinking of. The clues are often amusing with young children, as are the things that they choose to think about. The Thinking Game has many variations that need to be worked out prior to playing. It is a good game for changing and experimenting with rules. The game can be played anywhere and doesn't require any special equipment. Use the following steps to play The Thinking Game:

Step 1   Select someone to be *it*. Unlike playing tag, in The Thinking Game you want to be *it*. This person gets to determine the rules. They can take input from the other players, but they have the final say.

Step 2   Help *it* decide on the rules of the thinking game. You, or another adult might want to be *it* first to give the children an example. There are several rules for *it* to determine. Think about the following possibilities for rules and choose the ones you like. You can add others as you need them. Make sure all of the rules are clear before the game begins.

> 1. *It* decides what he/she is thinking about, writes it down, and tells the other players the category of things he/she is thinking about.
>   *Example: I'm thinking of "types of birds".*
> 2. *It* must give at least three clues before anyone guesses.
> 3. Who gets to guess first, second, third, etc. is decided by *it*.
> 4. After five clues without a correct guess *it* wins.
> 5. Anyone guessing the *"thing"* wins and gets to be *it*.

Step 3   Take turns being *it*. Make sure that *it* really gets to decide the rules. If the rules are not good, it will be clear and the next person to be *it* can change them. Talk about the rules between games. Which rules make the game fair? Which make it fun? Which make it difficult?

Part 2- Family Meetings

Step 1   Find a time and place to have a family meeting. Family meetings should be held at a time when all family members can be present and can commit at least thirty minutes of time. Make it clear to all family members that they are expected to be at the family meeting. If members cannot be present, reschedule the meeting.

Step 2   At the beginning of the family meeting tell everyone how the meeting will be run. Make it clear that everyone will have a turn to speak, only one person can speak at a time, and no one will be criticized for what they say. Set the agenda for the meeting. This does not have to be a formal agenda, but you should explain the purpose for the meeting and what is going to be discussed. The

family meeting for this chapter should be about family rules. You might set the agenda for the meeting by saying: *"We are going to have a short meeting to talk about the family rules. We want to know how they are working, and what might be changed to work better."* Ask if there are any questions and begin.

Step 3 The meeting on family rules might begin with a list of the family rules. Ask the children to list what they think are the family rules. This exercise will be interesting in itself. After you have listed the family rules, vote on three rules to talk about. Remember, everyone has a vote. Get suggestions from the children about how the rules are working and how they might be changed. Try to think of ways that rules might be changed and improved. Use rules that are working well as examples and a format for changing other rules.

Step 4 At some point you must make decisions about the rules being discussed. This might be done at the meeting, or at a later time. Information from family meetings should be *"advisory"* to parents. That is, parents should be the ultimate judge of what is the family rule and what is not. However, to give the meetings credibility parents should try to make changes in rules in response to good ideas. Remember, don't be afraid to try new approaches to old problems.

Chapter 8
Stress

One of the basic problems with parenting is that it is a full-time job, done on a part-time basis, with no pay. If being a parent were all that an adult had to worry about, the job would still be difficult -- but manageable. Parents, however, have countless things in their lives that compete with being a parent. Innumerable demands on time, energy, and money interfere with the quality of parenting, even though most parents would agree that the responsibilities of parenthood come first in their lives.

Parent's Stress

Most parents do well with their children when they have the time, money, and energy to invest. Unfortunately, many other aspects of adult life put demands on these expendable resources and influence the amount left over for our children. Careers, relationships with spouses and other adults, and housework are just a few aspects of adult life that compete with the time, energy, and money that is available to invest in our children.

Some would argue that it does not matter how much of any of these resources they spend on their children. They argue that it is quality not quantity. Well, it is not that simple. Even if it were true that quality -- not quantity -- is most important, what quality is there in interactions that are rushed because there is not enough time? What quality of interactions are there at a dinner table when there is not enough food for a decent meal? What quality is there when parents are so tired from work that they doze off while their child reports the highlights of the day. The quantity and quality of interactions is affected by the resources (time, energy, and money) available to families.

Time Time is perhaps the most valuable and scarce resource necessary for successful parenting, especially with recent increases in dual career families and single parenting. It is common

for a working couple or single parent, living in a large urban area with a preschool aged child, to find themselves spending less than three waking hours with their child. And nearly two of these hours are spent feeding, dressing, and undressing this child. A typical working parent schedule in a metropolitan area might look like this.

6:15-6:45 -	Arise and prepare for work. Child may be awake, but parents basically use this time to dress for work.
6:45-7:00 -	Quick breakfast for parents and child.
7:00-7:15 -	Help child dress for school/child care and get child's belongings ready.
7:15-8:00 -	45 minute commute to work including leaving child at school/childcare.
8:00-5:00 -	Work.
5:00-6:00 -	Pick up child and commute home.
6:00-7:00 -	Prepare and eat dinner.
7:00-8:00 -	Quality time.
8:00-8:15 -	Bath and Bed.

Such a schedule assumes that other necessities like grocery shopping, maintaining the home, and attending to adult relationships are taken care of between 8:15 p.m. and 6:15 a.m. Even so, there is still that quality time between 7:00 p.m. and 8:00 p.m. But, what happens to that time when you consider constraints on energy and money?

Energy My energy level at 7:00 p.m. after a full day of work is not very impressive. On an easy winter day my children want to spend time reading books and talking about the events of the day. On a tough summer day, it is soccer in the backyard against my two children and five other neighborhood kids. It is these soccer days that will convince you that parent-child relations, are affected by energy limits as much as time constraints.

Money Finally, lack of money plays a significant role in our relations with our children. It does so in several ways. The most obvious being the inability to provide the basics for a family. Being without food and clothing are, of course, detrimental to family life and parenting. There are also more subtle ways that the lack of money affects interactions. If parents are constantly worrying about money and how they will pay the bills, it is difficult to focus

on children and their needs. And, if parents are regularly put in the financial position of having to deny children the things that they really want (clothes, toys, or an occasional trip to the movies) they begin to feel inadequate in their ability to provide for their children, and their confidence as parents is shaken. These feelings of inadequacy are not overlooked by children.

Effects of Stress

In general, lack of resources creates stress in families that has a negative impact on the way they work. This affects both parental and child stress. Parents experience the direct consequences of not having enough time, energy, or money to feel comfortable in their role as parents and it is stressful. Children, on the other hand, experience the lack of these resources indirectly. Parents who are rushed, tired, and/or broke are not likely to have the highest quality interactions with their children. Many children will not fully understand that their parents are rushed, tired, and/or broke, but they will experience the effect of their parents' lack of resources through their interactions. This can create stressful situations for children.

Stress in parents and children can interfere with their relationships in several specific ways. First, the best planned strategies of parenting can fall apart in stressful times. Take any of the parenting issues discussed in Chapters 1,2, or 4. Discipline, communication, and gathering information can all be adversely affected by stress.

Discipline Consistency in discipline is a good illustration of the potential impact of stress. Consider the following scenario. Mom comes home from work at 6:00 p.m. tired, hungry, upset about a recent argument with the boss, and rushes to make dinner before a 7:00 p.m. meeting. Mom's four-year-old is sitting on the floor marking every page of a lovely picture book with a bright red crayon. Mom knows that the child is aware of the house rule against destroying books, but she is so stressed out that she decides not to tackle this one. Her child is quiet and not in the way, and she just cannot handle the thought of a major confrontation about the book.

Or, consider a different situation. Another mother comes home in the same stressful state. She walks into her eight-year-old child's room and finds a pair of shoes out of the closet. She blows up and makes the child *"stay in this room until it is spotless,"* but the room was already relatively clean, even by Mom's standards. Had

it not been for Mom's stress, the shoes would have been acceptable on the floor where they were left.

The result of stress in both these situations is inconsistent discipline. A consistent and fair system of discipline falls apart when our reactions to events are based upon uncontrolled emotions that are displayed because of high stress.

Communication Effective communication is also affected by stress. It is very difficult for me to take the time to listen to both sides of an argument between my daughters when I have just entered the door after a hectic day at work. I usually think of the easiest, most time efficient way to get them quiet. Something like, *"Why don't you girls just go outside and try to work it out."* In reality, they probably are telling <u>me</u> their story because they have not been able to work it out.

Available time and energy effects how much we communicate with our children, but it also effects the type of communication in which we engage. For example, rational well conceived conversations are most likely to occur when both parents and children are well rested and unrushed. Leisurely discussing the events of the day requires time and energy. On the other hand, when there is a shortage of time and energy, discussions are likely to be terse, and based on emotion rather than logic or rational thinking. Effective communication requires clear, logical presentations of information.

Gathering Information Getting the right information on the behaviors of children is obviously affected by stress. Stressed out parents are likely to overlook critical behaviors that their children are displaying. Both positive and negative behaviors can be easily overlooked when a parent is tired, worried, hungry, or in a hurry. Negative behaviors are especially sensitive to being overlooked during periods of high stress. Particularly if knowing about the behavior is going to require some type of action on the parents' part. That is, if parents recognize behaviors that are violating family rules, in the interest of consistency they need to respond. But responding to these violations requires time and energy, and if parents have exhausted their supply of time and energy, they may feel better overlooking or not noticing the broken rule.

Children's Stress

Parents need to become good managers of stress. Specific strategies that can be used to reduce stress and the subsequent impact that it has on the family will be presented later in this chapter. But, in addition to dealing with their own stress levels, parents need to be aware of the stress that their children experience.

Children experience a variety of stressors that are not always the same as those experienced by their parents. While children may occasionally be affected by time and energy constraints, they are not influenced by the lack of these resources to the same extent as adults. They are, however, stressed by a variety of other factors.

Pressures to Perform and Conform Perhaps the biggest of these stressors are the pressures to perform and conform. Young children are often pressured into higher and higher levels of performance, and are expected to conform to standards of behavior that get progressively more rigorous. This pressure may come from parents, teachers, their peers, or from themselves. Children who are constantly pressured to perform above their capabilities run the risk of burn-out or dramatic emotional responses to these pressures.

Observe a child learning to swim. It is a skill where children make rapid progress. However, for every skill that they master, their parents' expectations increase to include two or three new skills. Once a six-year-old learns to swim the width of the pool free-style, you become eager for her to learn to swim the breast stroke for the entire length. Parents tend to adapt and increase their expectations as soon as they observe that prior expectations have been met. This process, when it evolves gradually, is a very positive aspect of development. Children tend to rise to meet the expectations of their parents or teachers. That is, as long as the expectations are realistic. Once our increasing expectations outdistance our children's capability or desire, stress results.

Pressures to perform or conform, sometimes result in a fear of failure in children. Fear of failing and fear in general can be very stressful for young children. Some young children experience a variety of fears that go undiscovered throughout most of their lives. There is a negative stigma associated with being afraid that can put children in very vulnerable high stress situations. Sometimes this stigma comes out directly when parents interact with their children, and sometimes the stigma is more subtle.

When parents do not fully understand the extent of their children's fears they can pass them off as insignificant or trivial. The parent who proclaims, *"There's nothing to be afraid of!"*, and does not explain further is directly suppressing their child's future expressions of fear. Parents indirectly affect fear as well. A parent who praises a sibling for not being afraid in a potentially frightening situation puts an enormous amount of pressure on the other child who might be afraid. And, for all the parent knows, the child who did not express their fears was just as afraid, but better able to hide it.

Many children would like to talk about their fears, but are afraid of being ridiculed, or not taken seriously. Continued exposure to fearful situations can create considerable stress.

Reducing Stress

So what can be done to reduce stress in children and their parents? There are several approaches that families can adopt to manage stress. The first is to be aware and prepared. The more you are aware of the events in your family's life that are producing stress for both parents and children, the better able you are to prepare a plan for dealing with these stressful situations.

Be Prepared If you know that time is going to be tight, prepare in advance by being better organized and efficient. If you are aware that energy is going to be low, do not add additional strenuous activities to the schedule. Understanding when there are potentially stressful situations, and responding by changing the environment is essential to coping with stress.

Relax Expectations In addition to being aware and prepared to deal with stressful situations parents can help reduce stress in their children by altering their expectations. Lightening up on performance standards might be a good place to start. We all have expectations for our children that play a major role in their accomplishments. We should continue to help children set goals for themselves, but we should also be careful to assess how much stress each goal puts on children. A nine-year-old who sincerely believes (with a lot of help from his parents) that his only goal in life is to play in the Super Bowl is creating a number of potentially stressful situations for himself. Parents could help this child develop more achievable goals (like making the pee-wee team) that might eventually lead to more grand accomplishments. Setting

performance standards too high and pushing children to reach these goals creates considerable stress.

Communication   Another coping strategy is related to communication. Periods of high stress require particularly good communication. Listening and expressing yourself accurately can help buffer some of the effects of stressful periods. When you are tired, broke or hungry you should let your family know. Maybe the kids would even give you a break and not scream in your ear for thirty minutes or so. Try saying something like, *"Kids, this is really not the time for you to be aggravating me."* Interpreted, this means *"I'm tired (and/or rushed) and I'm not going to be nearly as tolerant as I am most of the time."* Wise children will respond by staying out of the way until it looks like a less stressful time. Furthermore, go beyond telling children that it is *"not the time,"* and tell them why it is not the time. It does not hurt to admit that you are under some stress and not nearly as tolerant as usual. At least children begin to understand those things that affect the behavior of their parents.

Understanding   Most importantly, periods of stress require compassion and empathy. Family members need to be taught to be sympathetic to the stress experienced by other members of the family. Understanding that stressful situations influence the behavior of your fellow family members is an important first step in helping these family members deal with their stressors. Support from family members is essential in coping with stress.

Consequently, when more than one family member is experiencing stress, the overall effect on the family is much more severe. Imagine returning home after a long and strenuous car trip. Everyone is tired, and everyone is stressed from the long, exhausting trip. The potential for a family conflict is high. Recognizing that these situations are particularly stressful, parents can either avoid them, or be sensitive to the behaviors that are affected by the stress and not react severely. It is difficult to avoid stress. But, with careful planning and compassion, you can minimize its effects on your family.

Activities for Chapter 8

After reading the story ask your child the following questions. Remember to give your child plenty of time to come up with answers, and to add your own thoughts.

1. What did Abear do wrong?

After giving your child time to come up with answers, point out that Abear:
   a. Left Weebear alone.
   b. Did not listen to his parents.
   c. Didn't try to help his parents when they were trying very hard to get food.

2. Why do you think Abear did what he did?

Point out that:
   a. Abear really wanted to spend time with Bearly.
   b. Abear did not think it was fair to have to stay home with Weebear.
   c. Abear was very bored.

3. Did Abear try to understand Mom and Dad's feelings?

Point out that Mom and Dad were tired and hungry and really were not paying attention to Abear and his needs. Abear was not paying attention to Mom and Dad's needs either. Talk about family responsibilities and everyone helping.

4. What could Abear have done differently?

   a. Abear could have stayed home with Weebear.
   b. Abear could have asked Dad how long he was going to be home.
   c. Abear could have found something fun to do and invited Bearly to stay at his house and help watch Weebear.

5. What could Mom and Dad have done differently?

   a. Mom and Dad could have talked to Abear about how important it was to watch Weebear.
   b. They could have told Abear when they would return, and that only then could he go with Bearly.
   c. They could have taken turns looking for food and stayed home to help watch Weebear.

Art Activity

Draw a picture of what happens next in the story. Finish the chapter. Follow one of these options:

  a. You and your child can draw a picture together.
  b. You and your child can draw your own pictures and the compare them.

Whether you draw a picture together or separately be sure to keep an ongoing discussion of the things being drawn. Have your child tell the end of the story using the picture that was drawn.

Parent Homework

Step 1   Identify particularly stressful times in your family. This might be when you first arrive home from work, at the end of the month when money is short, at bedtime, or any other time. Look for the source of stress in these situations. Are you or your children tired, hungry, broke, or worried? Are there other pressures that are influencing your behavior?

Step 2   Choose one of these stressful times and think of a new way to respond in these situations. Use one of the suggestions presented in this chapter to make the stressful situation more pleasant. Try more clear communication, being prepared, reducing your expectations, or simply encouraging family members to be more understanding.

Step 3   Don't spend alot of time on this homework assignment. In learning to manage stress you need to decide what is most important in terms of your time, energy, and income. You have spent considerable time and energy reading this book and going through the assignments. Hopefully, you have learned a thing or two and have practiced some new skills. Now it's time to take care of yourself. Decide what works for you and what doesn't. Use those things that work, and take it easy on yourself . Be good to yourself and it will be easier to be good to your children.